ENDORSEMENTS

Michael Sabo offers a practical blueprint for life in Christ against the backdrop of misinformation and relativism. Sabo weaves in captivating stories from his own life and from many others to illustrate, with clarity, much-needed sound theology and doctrine that help believers navigate guilt, fear, anxiety, loneliness, and more. I know this book will encourage and renew you, as it did me.

Lorden Chang, The Navigators

When emotions feel overwhelming or disorienting, Sabo guides readers back to the foundational promises and truths of Scripture. In doing so, he reorients the will, feelings, and freedom through abiding in Christ. Through this process, feelings can be in the service of spiritual discernment and wisdom. The book offers practical reflections and helpful suggestions for daily application.

Jon S. Ebert, PsyD, Clinical Psychologist HSP
Vanderbilt University Medical Center
Associate Professor of Clinical Psychiatry and Behavioral Sciences

Michael Sabo has done us a great service in clearly articulating the spiritual freedom God has provided for us in Jesus Christ. Using Scripture as the infallible map, Michael leads us on a journey that takes us from our new position of freedom as Christians to the practical outworking of this freedom in our everyday lives as we seek freedom from fear, guilt, pride, anger, loneliness, and anxiety. Michael gives us a fresh and motivating vision of the "freedom for which Christ set us free" (Gal. 5:1). You will see the Lord, yourself, and your own past and current struggles in a new and liberating light.

Lance Gentry, Senior Pastor
Cross & Crown Church, Colorado Springs, Colorado

In this carefully crafted book, Michael Sabo faithfully adheres to the foundational truths of our faith while pastorally navigating the feelings that often cloud our thinking. Those who desire to "live in the freedom Christ has already given them" will find a clear path laid out in that direction through these pages.

Jon Gilmore, Pastor of Music Ministry,
Cross & Crown Church, Colorado Springs, Colorado

Today, many believers strive to live holy lives in their own strength, not understanding how their position in Christ empowers them to practically and victoriously work out the gospel day by day for the glory of God. Michael helpfully teaches us how to preach the gospel to ourselves each day and to root our obedience in the finished work of Christ through his life, death, resurrection, and ascension. I highly recommend this to every believer who desires to live a holy life for God's glory!

Linda Green, former Women's Ministry Director and leader in
discipleship

Michael Sabo's book *Living in the Freedom of the Truth* not only offers a clear and concise picture of what keeps us in bondage, but also an effective biblical prescription plan on how its truth can sever its grip on us.

Ron Green, Professional Nature, Wildlife, and Scenic Photographer

In *Living in the Freedom of the Truth*, Michael Sabo addresses what is necessary to experience true freedom across multiple domains. He utilizes personal experiences, practical insight, helpful resources, and, most importantly, biblical support for his claims about one's ability to embody liberty. To recommend a work like this, the first three aspects are important; however, to highly recommend it, sound biblical undergirding is vital. This book is wholeheartedly recommended based on the inclusion of all four elements!

Dennis Hughes, MA, LPCC

Dr. Sabo provides us with a practical, yet gentle, approach to overcome guilt, anxiety, pride, fear, anger, and loneliness by applying God's truth to our lives. Always with the heart of a teacher, he makes sure the reader understands the biblical foundations (the Why) first, then gives an accessible way to apply this knowledge (the How) to grow in personal holiness. This book will be useful for pastors, counselors, parents, and individuals who want to grow and help others grow in their faith.

Stephen P. Street, MDiv, MA, LPC

A spiritual outfitter and guide, in one heart; that's what this author is. Dr. Sabo's *Living* book helps you get your gear in order for long-distance walking and living...with Jesus Christ: good shoes, water, outfit, hat, etc. Using stories, personal experiences, movies, dozens of pertinent and useful Scriptures, and even a suggested song that ties in to his themes, Mike guides any reader of this book into God's Word for the essentials and perspectives that are key to triumphing over our baggage that hinders living with the Savior.

Ken Valles, Founder of Karate Plus Ministries and KP Chronicles (using Christian karate and history stories to glorify God)

Dr. Sabo has gifted the Christian community with a thorough and readable exposition of "freedom in Christ." Insights derived from biblical and theological sources, combined with practical examples of freedom in Christ lived out, make this book a treasure. Christians everywhere will benefit greatly by reading this book and making its content their own.

**The Rev. Dr. Keith P. Wells
Professor Emeritus of Theological Research, Denver Seminary**

Michael has given me a much better understanding about how knowing and accepting who we are in Christ can help us to practically live out our faith, not according to our fickle feelings and past failures, but rather by focusing on the truths in God's Word that encourage and exhort us to press on to the end of our race, by the power of the Holy Spirit. I highly recommend this book to all who desire to walk unhampered in the freedom of God's truth!

**Terri Bache-Wiig, member of Cross & Crown Church
Colorado Springs, Colorado**

LIVING IN THE FREEDOM OF THE TRUTH

Are You Driven by Feelings or Drawn by Truth?

MICHAEL FRANK SABO

Publisher Information:
Michael Frank Sabo
Christian Leadership Institute
1439 N. Foote Ave.
Colorado Springs, CO 80909

For more information or to contact the author, please email cli-mfs@msn.com
website: https://christianleadership.institute

ISBN 979–8-9942471–1-2 (softcover)
ISBN 979–8-9942471–0-5 (hardcover)
ISBN 979–8-9942471–2-9 (eBook)

Cover design: Terry Dugan
Cover photo credit: Dilok @ Adobe Stock
Editorial team: Dr. Mark Tuggle, Penny Tuggle, and Cristina Wright
Interior design: Ben Wolf, Inc.
Publishing services provided by BelieversBookServices.com

First printing: 2026
Printed in the United States of America

CONTENTS

ACKNOWLEDGMENTS

While writing this book, I was reminded of the wisdom in Proverbs 24:6: "In the abundance of counselors there is salvation." In my case, the Christian community's abundance enabled me to write this book. Asking others to weigh in and help me has strengthened my relationship with each of you, led me to thank God for you by name, and resulted in a better book. In gratitude, I want to thank you by name.

My Lord: We both know this book would not exist without your love, mercy, and grace, lavishly poured out in my life. You surprised me with the opportunity to write it, and the writing process has deepened our communion. May it bring You great glory and help everyone who reads it live in the freedom of Your truth. Thank you, Lord.

My Wife: **Darlene**, thank you for loving and respecting me as we journey through life together. As you know, much of this book reflects what you and I have learned and experienced together. Your support, sacrifice, kindness, patience, and encouragement have been—and remain—a model of Christ for me. Thank you!

My Church Family: **Lance Gentry**, your leadership, pulpit teaching, and godly example continue to encourage me to deny myself and follow Jesus. I sincerely appreciate your kind words about this book—thank you.

Jon Gilmore, your leadership in our Sunday worship services lifts my heart in praise, drawing me into spiritual communion and worship of our triune God. In addition, your encouraging advice has made my book better—thank you.

Ray and Linda Green, I admire your perseverance with the Lord and your pinpoint, extraordinary insights that made this a better book —thank you.

Ron and Cori Green, my good friends, whom I so appreciate for your authentic walk with the Lord and the perceptive advice you gave on this book—thank you.

Terri Bache-Wigg, my sister in the Lord, whose attention to detail and astute observations have made this a higher-quality book— thank you.

My Good Friends: Lorden Chang, my faithful brother, who walked with me through a dark valley we both experienced, and from whom the Lord received our praise. I so appreciate your honest feedback and direction on the book—thank you.

Jon Ebert, my knowledgeable friend and son of my best friend, who is now in heaven, your advocacy and perceptive suggestions for this book were joyfully welcomed—thank you.

Dennis Hughes, a man of integrity and wisdom, read this book with careful attention and shared judicious, refined insights that were incredibly helpful in improving it—thank you.

Steve Street, a loyal and unwavering friend, is dedicated to the Lord and faithful in helping the saints. I greatly appreciate your sage and faultless guidance, which made my writing more practical—thank you.

Ken Valles, a faithful spiritual warrior and fellow martial artist, has been a great example to me, both on the mat and in how you persevere through life's trials. Your faultless, well-informed perspective on my writing endeavor has been invaluable—thank you.

Keith Wells, your long-term friendship in life and on the racquet-ball court will not be forgotten. I deeply appreciate your scholarly insights into the Bible, which made this book easier to understand— thank you.

My Editors and Designers: Thanks to the publishing team at **Believers Book Services**. I want to thank **Dave Sheets** for encouraging and helping me get moving in the right direction. Thanks to my friend **Marcus Costantino** for suggesting I write a book and for his help with the guidelines for writing and communicating what God has given me. Thanks so much to **Roberta Nichols** for her ongoing guidance and for quickly providing practical insights into the writing and publishing process. Thanks to **Terry Dugan** for his beautiful cover design, which honors God and clearly conveys the intent of my book. Also, gratitude to **Cristina Wright** for her thorough proofreading, and a special thanks to my good friends, **Mark and Penny Tuggle,** who spent multiple hours refining and editing my book. Your meticulous work made the book easier to read and understand. Finally, I want to thank **Justin Shreeves** for his expertise in interior layout and **Ben Wolf** for his guidance on online sales.

INTRODUCTION: THE BASIS
OF CHRISTIAN FREEDOM

So Jesus was saying to those Jews who had believed Him, "If you abide in My word, then you are truly My disciples; and you will know the truth, and the truth will make you free."
John 8:31–32

All Christians have an obligation to be students of truth. In fact, we are called to develop a love affair with the truth. It is ultimately truth, not knowledge or skill, that sets us free and makes us wholly creative. *Truth* is a strong word. There is something almost numinous about it. We should not speak of it lightly or casually.

Knowledge is quite different. It is something we can gain, something we can control, and something we can use. Knowledge, when we gain control of it, becomes ours, and we profit from its acquisition of it. Truth is another matter. Truth should gain and control us instead of being controlled by us. There is an element of unrelenting moral demand in truth; it is other-centered. It matters not whether we have mastered truth and can use it; it matters only whether we have surrendered to truth and are willing to obey it.[i]

To understand the basis of Christian freedom and this entire book, I briefly explain what the terms *word*, *truth*, and *free* mean in John 8:31–32.

Word

When Jesus uses the term *word* (*lógos*), He refers to Himself. He says, "I AM the living Word of God" (John 1:1). Therefore, when Jesus speaks, His words are fundamentally different in nature and origin from the Jews' understanding of the Scriptures and perhaps our understanding today. There is more to Jesus as the Word of God than the Bible's content. He invites us to an intimate, experiential relationship with the Living God, the very goal of Paul's passion in Philippians 3:7–10. As Jesus says, we must abide (constant, intimate communion) in His Word (in Him, John 15:1–11), for this is a fundamental need for all of Jesus' disciples.

Truth

When Jesus uses the term *truth* (*alḗtheia*), He refers to Himself and the reality of the universe He created. God alone knows and sees everything perfectly, as it really is. Divine truth includes not only what is real but also declares the existence and will of the triune God of the universe. As Jesus' disciples abide in Him, they will have an experiential encounter with truth. They will not only have more biblical doctrine in their minds but also know (experience) Jesus more intimately (John 14:6, 21).

Free

When Jesus uses the term *free* (*eleutheróō*), He refers to liberation from enslavement to sin, from eternal punishment for sin, and from all the bondage that sin entails.

In summary, Jesus says that if we remain in constant communion with Him, who is the Word and truth, we will experience a transforming, eternal freedom from sin's enslavement, punishment, and bondage.

Free on the Inside

As indicated in the dedication, a close friend of mine is serving time in prison for a crime he did not commit. Having worked in the criminal justice system as a deputy warden, a prison counselor, and later as a probation and parole officer, I am well aware of the injustices within the courts. Two reasons for this are, first, that the judge lacks the ability to know the thoughts and intentions of the person on trial. Therefore, the judge must rely on the prosecution and defense to reveal the truth. Second, we all know this system, despite being the best we have, is a system of law rather than justice and is seriously flawed due to the limitations of judges, juries, and humanity.

It's not uncommon for someone who is guilty to get released because of a legal technicality. Guilty but free—a certain justice oxymoron. Additionally, I have observed individuals, such as my friend, who were found guilty not because of a just decision but because of strict adherence to the law, regardless of how unjust those rules might be. My friend is a solid, mature Christian who is outwardly restrained but remarkably free internally. A sophisticated security system, steel bars, and armed guards prevent him from leaving. He cannot escape or choose to overcome all that is in his way. But knowing him, if he had Superman's powers to bypass these physical obstacles, he wouldn't use them, because breaking out of prison is against the law—ironic.

Jesus is the One who, when He frees us from internal enslavement to sin, gives us the strength to learn, understand, and navigate the external restrictions in our world, enabling us to make different choices than those we would have made while internally imprisoned. Our being always influences our actions. But far more importantly, no matter how physically constrained my friend may be, he lives a free life on the inside. How? He has been freed by the work of Jesus on the cross. This doesn't mean he is never tempted by fear, anxiety, or sorrow; however, he has the God-given ability to choose to live in the truth despite his negative feelings. His choices are directly linked to the truth of God's Word.

The freedom Jesus has won for us is not the ability to do whatever we want. It is being enabled to be who God designed us to be (holy, 1 Peter 1:15–16) and to do the good works He created for us (Ephesians 2:10), nothing more and nothing less. However, to achieve the good works God intends for us, we must undergo an internal transformation and start growing in practical righteousness. Let's look to biblical history for an example.

Because of Israel's decision to pursue idols, they were about to reap what they had sown. God's people had exchanged the glory and majesty of the one true God for a false substitute. Their God loved, protected, and provided for them from Egypt to the present, yet they rejected the truth for a lie. Therefore, Yahweh was about to unleash the evil Babylonian army upon His own people—an enemy that the prophet Habakkuk declared was more wicked than Israel. Nevertheless, Israel chose to reject Yahweh and pursue something false. During Jeremiah's wait for the impending invasion, he cried out for Yahweh's mercy. In Jeremiah's prayer (10:23–25), we learn a humbling truth about our limitations: "I know, O Yahweh, that a man's way is not in himself, nor is it in a man who walks to direct his steps."

Jeremiah recognized that Yahweh was sovereign while humanity was not. He acknowledged that people cannot direct their lives apart from God (Psalm 37:23–24; Proverbs 3:5–6, 16:9, 19:21, 20:24). The prophet Habakkuk was not happy that God would use the Babylonians to punish Israel, but he understood Yahweh's punishment was just (Habakkuk 1:12–2:20, 3:1–19).

Based on their actions, these Jews believed they knew what was best for themselves and chose a path contrary to the truth (Proverbs 14:12). Their decision may have felt right, but it led to God's discipline. It is quite common for humanity—and sometimes for Christians—to forget that we have been made not only by God but also for God (Colossians 1:16; Romans 11:36). Since God created us for Himself, He wants what is best for us. Remember what Jeremiah said: "A man's way is not in himself, nor is it in a man who walks to direct his steps." Therefore, God commands us to "trust Him" rather than our own insights (Proverbs 3:5–6). Just like Israel, when we rely on ourselves, we sin and face the consequences.

So, what does all this have to do with freedom? Remember, freedom is not the ability to do what we want to do. It is being enabled to be who God designed us to be and to do the good works He created for us, nothing more and nothing less.

Being leads to doing. God commanded His followers to be holy, for He is holy (1 Peter 1:15–16). As we grow in practical (progressive) holiness, our beliefs, speech, and actions will become more holy. However, remember Jeremiah taught that we lack the ability within ourselves to live as God desires (10:23; Romans 7:18).

The apostle Paul, in his New Testament epistles, begins his letters by emphasizing doctrine and ends with its practical application. I will follow Paul's example by dividing this book into two sections. In the first section, we will closely examine the doctrines of positional and practical holiness. Although, as Christians, God has justified us (positional holiness) by granting us the righteousness and holiness of Jesus, our practical sanctification requires a freedom that relies on the Holy Spirit's help for growth; this is what we will explore in the second section.

We are told in Galatians 5:1, "It was for freedom that Christ set us free. Therefore, stand firm and do not be subject again to a yoke of slavery." In this verse, Paul states that the Galatians have been freed from the yoke (a form of bondage) of the law that required them to earn righteousness. The only way to live in this freedom is with the conviction that God's grace alone, through Jesus' work, is sufficient and complete for our salvation.

Not only does Christ free us from the bondage of the law, but His purpose is to liberate us from all forms of slavery. Bondage is used in many contexts around the world. In this book, I will refer to it as being hindered from living the life God intends for us—a life of freedom. In other words, whenever we are unable or unwilling to live as God desires, it constitutes a form of bondage. Bondage can manifest as external physical limitations or internal emotional struggles. However, I will focus on the internal bondage we can experience in various ways, which will be discussed in section two. In section one, we will see that internal bondage is linked to the choices we make, both consciously and unconsciously.

But this freedom in Galatians 5:1 isn't about doing whatever the Galatians wanted. Instead, it's about being and doing what the Lord created them to be and do—holy and righteous. We were set free to be holy in position and to do holy things in practice (righteousness) at our conversion.

However, the journey in our sanctification involves moving from bondage to freedom (Romans 6:17–19). God opposes any form of bondage that hinders His children from living a holy and righteous life by faith. Living a life of faith means not only choosing to obey the truth of Scripture but also being aware that the Holy Spirit will guide us to seek Him for wisdom and discernment (James 1:5, 3:17–18).

People who live by faith are guided by God's love for them (2 Corinthians 5:14), which in turn nurtures a growing love for God (Matthew 22:37–40). This mutual love encourages worship, service, and submission to whatever God has planned for our lives. Such a lifestyle cultivates divine freedom from within, achieved by choosing to live in truth. Living in freedom means not trying to earn our salvation through good works. Additionally, true freedom entails avoiding a life dominated by negative feelings. In other words, we can't fully experience freedom unless we choose to follow the Spirit, who will never lead us to do anything against God's Word. Simply put, a life that trusts God by obeying His truth in every experience, big or small, regardless of emotional ties, is genuinely a life of freedom. Deciding to live by trusting God's Word prevents inner bondage and allows us to experience the freedom Jesus gave us at our conversion.

Freedom requires self-denial; that denial depends on our choice, which is influenced by whether we rest on Jesus or our flesh (Matthew 7:24–27). Remember how the apostle Paul asked the Lord three times to remove his thorn (2 Corinthians 12:7–8)? Each time, Jesus answered no and said to Paul, "My grace is sufficient for you, for power is perfected in weakness" (2 Corinthians 12:9).

Following Jesus' words, we see that the apostle Paul *learned* to be content with his weaknesses: "Most gladly, therefore, I will rather boast in my weaknesses, so that the power of Christ may dwell in me. Therefore I am well content with weaknesses, with insults, with distresses, with persecutions and hardships, for the sake of Christ; for when I am weak, then I am strong" (vv. 9b–10). Paul's contentment was a choice, not an emotion. His contentment was directly linked to the purposes of Christ. Whatever glorified Jesus and served His purposes, Paul chose to accept because he understood he was created by Jesus and for Jesus.

Freedom is woven into every chapter of this book, and this freedom is intimately connected with truth. Anyone who embraces falsehood distances himself from Jesus, the One who declared Himself to be the Truth and the Bridegroom of the church. To turn away from Him or to accept anxiety or fear as truth is not only a form of deception but also an act of idolatry, which leads to further bondage.

Freedom is a choice. When we embrace our weaknesses as strengths in the presence of Jesus, we will surrender to His sovereign control. As we grow in practicing the truth, we will be set free from every kind of bondage. In chapter two, I will provide additional insight and clarity on the freedom of the will.

An essential principle in this book is that it is not the event or feeling itself, but rather our interpretation of it, that influences our lives. Our interpretation of any event or emotion must always be filtered through the truth of God's Word—nothing else. This process should serve as the standard pattern of our sanctification. In His High Priestly Prayer in John 17, Jesus prayed to His Father, "Sanctify them by truth; Your Word is truth" (v. 17). Please note that Jesus did not say, "Sanctify them in feelings; your word is feelings!"

Jesus tells us in John 14:6, "I am the way, and the truth, and the life." Notice, Jesus doesn't tell us He is the feeling but rather the truth. To live in truth is to have the mind of Christ (1 Corinthians 2:16), which enables us to avoid being held in the bondage of negative feelings. We cannot know the way without the truth, and we cannot live in freedom without the truth.

My purpose in this book is that we would bring glory to God (Isaiah 43:1–7) by living in the freedom He has already given us (Galatians 5:1). Be advised that the contents of chapters four through ten are not intended to be comprehensive but to offer brief yet truthful insights to help us get back on track and remain aligned with the truth (Psalm 25:5, 10).

I have divided the writing into two sections: "Part I: Biblical Foundations for Our Freedom" and "Part II: Biblical Living for Our Freedom." The chapter topics related to these sections are as follows:

Biblical Foundations for Our Freedom

1. Freedom Positionally and Practically
2. Freedom of the Will
3. Freedom Through a Renewed Mind

Biblical Living for Our Freedom

4. Freedom from Guilt
5. Freedom from Worry
6. Freedom from Pride
7. Freedom from Fear
8. Freedom from Unrighteous Anger
9. Freedom from Loneliness
10. Freedom to Worship God in Spirit and Truth

Negative feelings can lead us to focus on ourselves. While we cannot always avoid negative emotions and attacks, we can choose to prevent their persistent influence from affecting us. Chapters four through ten each examine a problematic feeling that can be transformed into an opportunity to deny self and glorify Jesus (Luke 9:23; Galatians 2:20). Beginning with this Introduction, and in each chapter and the Conclusion, I will present a biblical truth related to the topic at the start of each chapter and conclude with the following:

1. A suggested hymn or song to listen to when struggling with the chapter topic. For this Introduction, I encourage you to listen to "The Truth" by Megan Woods (August 2024).

2. Three small-group discussion questions related to the chapter topic.

3. Three suggestions for living in the truth when struggling with the chapter topic.

Part One

BIBLICAL FOUNDATIONS FOR OUR FREEDOM

This section presents the book's foundational truths. In other words, chapters one through three lay the doctrinal groundwork for understanding and living a life of freedom.

Chapter One

FREEDOM POSITIONALLY AND PRACTICALLY

*It was for freedom that Christ set us free. Therefore,
stand firm and do not be subject again to a yoke of slavery.*
GALATIANS 5:1

One afternoon, I sat on our back patio waiting for my daughter to return home from school, which I could see from our home. Just before I spotted her walking down the alley, the phone rang. When I answered, my daughter's teacher's pleasant voice delivered unwelcome news. "Mr. Sabo, just a few minutes ago, as your daughter was leaving my classroom, I noticed her take a bag of seashells that belonged to the school." Feeling disappointed, I asked the teacher how long she would be at the school so I could bring my daughter and the seashells to her. She assured me she would wait for us at the school. Once I ended the call, I saw my daughter walking up the alley with a small plastic bag containing seashells. When my daughter saw me, she ran to me with a big smile, yelling, "Daddy, Daddy, look what I found on the road!" I felt a very unpleasant sensation in my stomach.

As my daughter and I sat down at the picnic table, she poured out her newfound treasure onto the surface. Looking at the seashells, I said, "These really are nice seashells! Where did you say you got them?" An opportunity to live in truth resulted in living a lie. My little daughter replied, "Oh, I found them on the road, Daddy." (As I wrote this sentence, I reflected on how many times I had lied to others throughout my life.) I said to my daughter, "But that isn't where you got them, is it?" She quietly bowed her head and answered, "No, Daddy." "Where did you get them?" I inquired. Softly, she said, "I took them from the school." I then asked, "What must we do?" I wanted my daughter to understand that I didn't condemn her, and I would go with her to return the shells to her teacher. This time, she stayed quiet longer but then softly said, "We need to take them back, but I'm afraid, Daddy!" I assured her, "I know, but we will go together."

We then slowly walked the three-hundred-foot journey from our home to the school. My daughter held my finger with her little hand while clasping her sin in the other. I could see the fear on her face as we approached the school. I opened the door to the old elementary school, and it squeaked loudly, easily heard since all the kids were now gone. As we walked down the empty hallway, our footsteps echoed throughout the building. Suddenly, the teacher's door opened, and the teacher walked out about thirty feet in front of us. When my daughter made eye contact with her, she quickly dropped her head. But then the teacher did a beautiful thing. She dropped down on one knee, opened her arms wide, and called out my daughter's name, inviting her to come to her. When my daughter heard her name, she looked up and saw a big smile on her teacher's face, welcoming her into her arms. My daughter quickly ran to her teacher with her sin in hand. The teacher scooped up my daughter and spun her around in joy. When the teacher put my daughter back on the floor, my daughter gave her sin to the teacher and walked away free! This is a story I will never forget, because it reminds me of what Jesus did with me and my sin.

Because of Jesus' great love for us, this beautifully illustrates what He desires of us regarding our sin. He already knows what we have done; He knew it before we did. Yet, as His children, He invites us to bring our sins to Him. As we humbly confess, He joyfully wraps us in His arms, forgiving us (1 John 1:9), and reminds us of His love for us (Romans 8:37–39). It is God's love and kindness that can motivate us to live pure lives, free from any form of internal bondage (2 Corinthians 5:14; Romans 2:4). The King of the universe has adopted us as His children (Galatians 4:5–6; Ephesians 1:5) and, therefore, loves and forgives us because His mercies are new every morning (Lamentations 3:22–23).

Without diving into a detailed theological explanation, my goal in this first chapter is to clarify our positional and practical holiness in Christ. Understanding our permanent relationship with Christ can provide a strong foundation for our entire Christian life on earth, including how to respond to trials, suffering, and the negative feelings we all regularly experience. Therefore, I will start with the example of marriage and then connect what we learn about marriage to holiness. Just as marriage involves an event, a process, a state or condition, and a quality, holiness also has these aspects.

Marriage as an Event

What begins a marriage? It is, of course, the wedding. When a pastor pronounces a man and a woman husband and wife, they immediately become fully and legally bound together and cannot be more married.

Marriage as a Process

At the wedding, the couple not only becomes legally and positionally married but also immediately begins the practical aspects of their marriage. This is the everyday, real-life commitment they make to each other at their wedding.

Marriage as a State or Condition

When people fill out government forms and reach the section asking about their marital status, they are essentially being asked, "What is your marital state or condition?" Since they are married, they check the married box.

Marriage Quality

Every marriage journey involves learning to live with your spouse, whom you quickly realize is very different from you. This can easily lead to conflicts within the marriage. When the couple disagrees, they are still married, but the quality of their relationship may decline until the issue is resolved.

Now that we have briefly reviewed four aspects of marriage, I want to explore in more detail how these same four aspects relate to being holy unto the Lord. I will add two terms to each of the four aspects to clarify the different usages of holiness in the Bible as they relate to us. These two terms are *positional holiness* and *practical holiness*.

Using a chart, I have clearly outlined the key details of these four aspects. I will first list the details in the chart and then explain how they relate to our holiness.

ASPECT OF HOLINESS	POSITIONAL HOLINESS	PRACTICAL HOLINESS
Event	Secured at Conversion	Begins at Conversion
Process	Instantaneous	Completed in Glory
State or Condition	You are Holy	Depends On Whom You Abide In
Quality	Complete/Perfect	Increasing

The three headings of the chart are to be understood as follows: **Aspects of Holiness** include event, process, state or condition, and quality. As you can see, these are the same four I briefly reviewed regarding marriage. I will go on to explain how each of these applies to holiness in our lives. **Positional Holiness** refers to some of the privileges you received when you became a Christian. **Practical Holiness** refers to the practical activities involved in your daily sanctification.

ASPECT OF HOLINESS	POSITIONAL HOLINESS	PRACTICAL HOLINESS
Event	Secured at Conversion	Begins at Conversion

Event refers to your conversion, the moment you became a Christian.

Our POSITIONAL holiness was secured at our Conversion (EVENT). "Some of you were once like that. But you were cleansed; you were made holy; you were made right with God by calling on the name of the Lord Jesus Christ and by the Spirit of our God" (1 Corinthians 6:11, NLT).

Just as a wedding marks the beginning of a couple's union, both in a positional and practical sense, our conversion signifies a similar milestone. The moment we genuinely confessed with our mouth that Jesus is Lord and believed in our heart that God the Father raised Jesus from the dead, we were permanently saved (Romans 10:9–10) and became a new creation in Christ (2 Corinthians 5:17). In 1 Corinthians 6:11, Paul explains that, at their conversion, the Corinthians were washed, sanctified, and justified in Jesus and the Holy Spirit. Jesus' righteousness and holiness have been imputed to their account (Romans 3:21–22, 4:22; Philippians 3:9). Positionally, they are perfectly and completely holy because they have been regenerated—born again, made spiritually alive—by the Holy Spirit and granted eternal life (Titus 3:5; 2 Corinthians 5:17; Ephesians 2:10; John 3:3–8).

Our positional holiness and righteousness are complete and cannot be improved, even in heaven. When we were declared justified by God, it means that in Christ we have a new standing before Him. For when we believed, as stated in Romans 3:26, we were made right with God, and according to Romans 4:22–25, we were clothed in the righteousness of Christ. Additionally, as mentioned in 2 Peter 1:4, we became a partaker of the divine (holy) nature.

Our PRACTICAL holiness began at our Conversion (EVENT). "Now may the God of peace make you holy in every way and may your whole spirit and soul and body be kept blameless until that day when our Lord Jesus Christ comes again" (1 Thessalonians 5:23, NLT).

Just as a married couple's practical marriage begins at the wedding, so, too, does our sanctification begin at our conversion, reflecting the growing, practical, ongoing aspects of our holiness. At the event of our Christian life, we were made positionally holy, and with the help of the Holy Spirit, we will grow more righteous and holy in practice. Throughout Scripture, God has set apart many individuals in both the

Old and New Testaments for His purposes. These include Abraham, Moses, David, John the Baptist, Peter, and Paul. In 1 Thessalonians 5:23, Paul tells the Thessalonians that they, too, have been set apart for God's work, and so have we! Sanctification is the ongoing spiritual process in which the Holy Spirit guides us away from sin to perfect practical holiness, the goal of our sanctification.

Before becoming a Christian, we were unholy and unable to live a life that pleased God (Ephesians 2:1–3; Romans 3:10–18). However, at our conversion, we received a holy nature (positional, 2 Peter 1:4) and gained the power to grow in practical holiness through the sanctifying work of the Holy Spirit. We are no longer enslaved to sin and now have the choice to sin or not (1 Corinthians 10:13). I will share more details about this truth in chapter two on the Freedom of the Will.

ASPECT OF HOLINESS	POSITIONAL HOLINESS	PRACTICAL HOLINESS
Process	Instantaneous	Completed in Glory

Process refers to our daily sanctification.

The PROCESS of our POSITIONAL holiness was instantaneous. "For seven days you shall make atonement for the altar and set it apart as holy; then the altar shall be most holy, *and* whatever touches the altar shall be holy." (Exodus 29:37).

When a couple is married, they are legally united. But how quickly does the process of becoming legally married occur? It happens immediately. Essentially, the process of our positional holiness both started and was instantly achieved at the moment of our conversion. Exodus 29:37 shows that an offering becomes instantly holy upon contact with the holy altar, without any delay. In other words, when the Holy Spirit regenerated us, our sanctification began immediately.

The PROCESS of our PRACTICAL holiness will be completed in glory. "For by that one offering he perfected forever all those whom he is making holy" (Hebrews 10:14, NLT).

The process of marriage begins with the pronouncement of husband and wife and continues until the death of one of the spouses.

So, too, the process of our sanctification began at our conversion and continues until its completion in glory. According to 2 Corinthians 7:1, the journey of practical holiness involves our reverence for God, as reflected in our daily confession. Our goal of perfect practical holiness will be achieved at our glorification when we see Jesus face-to-face (1 John 3:2).

ASPECT OF HOLINESS	POSITIONAL HOLINESS	PRACTICAL HOLINESS
State or Condition	You Are Holy	Depends On Whom You Abide In

State or Condition refers to our present reality of holiness.

The state or condition of our positional holiness is the fact that we are holy. "We are writing to the Church of God in Corinth, you who have been called by God to be his own holy people. He made you holy by means of Christ Jesus, just as he did all Christians everywhere—whoever calls upon the name of Jesus Christ, our Lord and theirs" (1 Corinthians 1:2, NLT).

Positionally, God intends married couples to remain in a state or condition of marriage for as long as they live. The same applies to all Christians, who exist in a state or condition of holiness for eternity! This cannot change before we die or when we reach heaven (Romans 8:37–39; John 6:39–40, 10:28–29).

According to 1 Corinthians 1:2, all Christians are made positionally holy in Jesus. All Christians are saints (holy ones) by virtue of their spiritual birth, not by their works or by a religious organization granting them this status. Here, the Corinthian believers, despite their sinful lifestyles or incorrect doctrine, are considered holy in God's sight because of what Jesus has done in their lives. They hold a holy position just like the apostle Paul, and the same is true for us.

The state or condition of our practical holiness depends on whether we are abiding in Jesus or our flesh (John 15:5; Matthew 7:24– 27; Galatians 5:16–23). "If you keep yourself pure, you will be a special utensil for honorable use. Your life will be clean, and you will be ready for the Master to use you for every good work" (2 Timothy 2:21, NLT).

We can be married without truly living that way. Some people are legally married but act as if they are single. In other words, a gap can exist between our legal marriage status and our actual lifestyle. This discrepancy also relates to our practical holiness regarding our state or condition.

In 2 Timothy 2:21, we are told that to be used by God, we must be in a state or condition of practical holiness. This is achieved by cleansing ourselves of all sin through confession (1 John 1:9), thereby preparing for any good work Jesus has planned for us. In this context, Paul urges Christians to maintain their purity by avoiding false teachers, such as Hymenaeus and Philetus, who are blasphemers, as well as other teachers who have strayed from the truth. This is an important warning: the teachers (cultural influencers, entertainers, authors, podcasters, etc.) we listen to greatly impact our lives, and we are not only responsible for choosing them but also for verifying their message with Scripture (Acts 17:10).

ASPECT OF HOLINESS	POSITIONAL HOLINESS	PRACTICAL HOLINESS
Quality	Complete/Perfect	Increasing

Quality refers to the level of holiness in our lives.

The quality of our positional holiness is complete and perfect. "Long ago, even before he made the world, God loved us and chose us in Christ to be holy and without fault in his eyes" (Ephesians 1:4, NLT).

The positional quality of every marriage is perfect. In other words, legally, your marriage cannot become more married. At the moment of a marriage's pronouncement, the positional quality of the marriage is complete.

The positional quality of our holiness is perfect. We stand before God's throne in Christ, and by His grace, His righteousness and holiness have been imputed to us at our conversion, never to be changed in any way. The Apostle Paul tells the Corinthian Christians what has already happened to them (past tense) concerning their positional holiness in 1 Corinthians 6:11, "And such were some of you; but you were washed, but you were sanctified, but you were justified in the name of the Lord Jesus Christ and in the Spirit of our God." Paul declares that these Corinthian believers and all believers are positionally holy now and in heaven.

The quality of our practical holiness is increasing. "But now you must be holy in everything you do, just as God—who chose you to be his children—is holy. For he himself has said, 'You must be holy because I am holy'" (1 Peter 1:15–16, NLT). The Lord's intention for every marriage is practical growth in love and respect for one another (Genesis 2:18–24; 1 Corinthians 7:1–5; Ephesians 5:22–23; Colossians 3:18–19; 1 Peter 3:1–7; Hebrews 13:4).

In 1 Peter 1:15–16, the apostle Peter instructs Christians to be holy and live holy lives because God, who chose us to be holy, is Himself holy. With the help of the Holy Spirit, we have a responsibility to improve the quality of our practical holiness. However, our confidence should never rely solely on our own abilities. The apostle Paul assures us in Philippians 1:6, "For I am confident of this very thing, that He who began a good work in you will perfect it until the day of Christ Jesus." Rest assured that what the Holy Spirit started in our lives will be fulfilled, even in spite of our failures.

The quality of our practical holiness depends on what we abide in. According to Galatians 5:19–21, if we abide in our flesh (Matthew 7:26–27), the quality of our practical holiness will be nonexistent. But if we abide in Jesus (John 15:1–11), our practical holiness will flourish with fruitfulness (Galatians 5:22–23; Matthew 7:24–25). In other words, if we live by the Spirit, we will not fulfill the desires of the flesh (Galatians 5:16).

Trust in the promise of 1 John 3:2: "Beloved, now we are children of God, and it has not been manifested what we will be. We know that when He is manifested, we will be like Him, because we will see Him just as He is." The apostle John tells us that when we are fully glorified, we will be both positionally and practically holy, enjoying perfect and eternal communion with the Holy Trinity.

Using marriage as our example and starting point, I briefly reviewed holiness in the New Testament. All references pertain to us. Keep these distinctions in mind as you read the next two doctrinal chapters (two and three) of this book. The truth presented in these chapters empowers us against all enemies that confront us daily; this is the path to freedom. Remember how we began this chapter: "It was for freedom that Christ set us free. Therefore, stand firm and do not be subject again to a yoke of slavery" (Galatians 5:1).

Don't forget that freedom is not the ability to do whatever we want. It is being empowered to become who God designed us to be (1 Peter 1:15–16) and to do the good works He created for us (Ephesians 2:10; James 2:17–26), nothing more and nothing less.

I suggest taking the time to listen to the beautiful hymn "O the Deep, Deep Love of Jesus" by Samuel Trevor Francis (1875).

Small-Group Discussion Questions

1. To clarify your understanding, note some differences between the event, process, state/condition, and quality of your holiness.

2. Why are positional and practical holiness necessary for you to see Jesus face to face in heaven?

3. How can the event, process, state/condition, and quality of your holiness contribute to further growth in your Christian life?

Suggestions for Freedom Positionally and Practically

1. Praise God that at your conversion, you received perfect positional holiness, which can never be taken away.

2. Confess your sins to restore the practical quality of holiness in your life.

3. Memorize and regularly meditate on John 15:5.

Chapter Two

FREEDOM OF THE WILL

Trust in Yahweh with all your heart, and do not lean on your own understanding. In all your ways acknowledge Him, and He will make your paths straight.
PROVERBS 3:5–6

Bishop Augustine Hippo, also known as Saint Augustine (AD 354–430), once prayed, "Oh God, grant what thou dost command and command what thou dost desire." Pelagius (ca. AD 354–415), a British-born monk and Roman theologian, disagreed with Augustine's prayer. He believed anyone could obey God's law without assistance from God (grace) and, therefore, could earn salvation through good works. Pelagius founded what is now known as Pelagianism, which was condemned as heresy at the Council of Carthage in AD 418 and again at the Council of Ephesus in AD 431.

Pelagius sparked a major theological debate with Saint Augustine over sin, grace, and salvation. Pelagius rejected the doctrines of original sin and predestination and believed that humans were born with free will, unhindered by Adam's original sin. Therefore, he believed humans were fully capable of doing good on their own without any help from God. As a result, he took issue with Augustine's prayer.

Pelagius raised these questions: Is the assistance of grace necessary for a human being to obey God's commands? Or can these commands be obeyed without such assistance? For Pelagius, the command to obey implied the ability to obey. This would be true not only of the moral law of God, but also of the commands inherent in the gospel. If God commands people to believe in Christ, then they must have the power to believe in Christ without the aid of grace. If God commands sinners to repent, they must have the ability to incline themselves to obey that command. Obedience does not, in any way, need to be "granted."[i]

How Does the Will Function?

To further explain how our will functions, I have selected multiple quotations from Jonathan Edwards' book *Freedom of the Will* (1754) as recorded in R. C. Sproul's book *Willing to Believe: The Controversy over Free Will* (1997).

I have numbered these quotes to make each point easier to consider.

1. Edwards defines the will as "that by which the mind chooses anything."[ii]

2. "Edwards argues that will and desire are not 'so entirely distinct, that they can ever be properly said to run counter. A man never, in any instance, wills anything contrary to his desires, or desires anything contrary to his will.' This means that man always acts according to his desire. Edwards indicates that the determining factor in every choice is the 'strongest motive' present at that moment. In summary, we always choose according to the strongest motive or desire at that time."[iii]

3. "Our desires are often complex and even in conflict with each other. Even the apostle Paul experienced conflicting desires, claiming that what he wanted to do he failed to do and what he did not want to do he actually did (Romans 7:15). Paul does not disagree with Edwards, rather he expresses the struggle between desires in conflict."[iv]

4. "Every time a Christian sins, at that moment, he desires the sin more than obeying God. If not, we wouldn't sin." [v]

5. According to R. C. Sproul, our desires are not constant in their force or intensity. Our desire levels fluctuate from moment to moment. Sproul gives the following two examples: [vi]
   a. "The dieter desires to lose weight. After a full meal it is easy to say no to sweets. The appetite has been sated and the desire for more food diminished. As time passes, however, and self-denial has led to an increased hunger, the desire for food intensifies. The desire to lose weight remains. But when the desire to gorge oneself becomes stronger than the desire to lose weight, the dieter's resolve weakens and he succumbs to temptation. All things do not remain in a constant state of equality." [vii]
   b. "A robber holds a gun to your head and says, give me your money or your life. Most people will opt to give their money reasoning that, if I don't give him my money, he will both kill me and take my money. However, it is possible that the victim would prefer to die rather than give over his wallet 'willingly.'" [viii]

6. "Under these coercive circumstances, is either choice voluntary? It is if we view it in the context of only two options."[ix]

7. "Even though external coercion is involved, there still remains a choice. Even here, Edwards would say, the person will choose the alternative for which he or she has the stronger motive. What about the seat you chose to sit in without giving it any conscious thought? Even in this situation, there are subtle preferences or motives operating."[x]

8. "Your choice was voluntary; it was not involuntary like the beating of your heart."[xi]

What Determines Our Choices?

Here again, we can turn to Sproul's observations of Edwards' work.

1. "Our will's choices are directed to and fixed upon a particular object." [xii]

2. "If the will be determined, there is a determiner."[xiii]

3. "Edwards argues from the *law of cause and effect,* which says, for every effect there is an antecedent cause."[xiv]

4. "The will is always determined by the strongest motive. Edwards further argues that the strongest motive is that which appears most 'good' or 'pleasing' to the mind. Here, he uses good not in the moral sense, because we may be most pleased by doing what is not good morally. Rather, the volition acts according to that which appears most agreeable to the person. That which is most pleasing may be deemed as pleasure. What entices fallen man to sin is the desire for some perceived pleasure.[xv]

5. "Given man's moral inability, the will cannot not be free. The will is always free to act according to the strongest motive or inclination at the moment. *For Edwards, this is the essence of freedom* (emphasis added). To be able to choose what one desires is to be free in this sense. *When I say the will cannot not be free, I mean the will cannot choose against its strongest inclination* (emphasis added). It cannot choose what it does not desire to choose. Edwards refers to the common meaning of *liberty*: 'that power and opportunity for one to do and conduct as he will, or according to his choice.'" [xvi]

6. "A summary of Edward's view of original sin: Man is morally incapable of choosing the things of God unless or until God changes the disposition of his soul. Man's moral inability is due to a critical lack and deficiency, namely, the motive or desire for the things of God. Left to himself, man

will never choose Christ. He has no inclination to do so in
his fallen state. Since he cannot act against his strongest
inclination, he will never choose Christ unless God first
changes the inclination of his soul by the immediate and
supernatural work of regeneration. Only God can liberate
the sinner from his bondage to his own evil
inclinations."[xvii]

7. "Like Augustine, Luther, and Calvin, Edwards argues man
    is free in that he can and does choose what he desires or is
    inclined to choose. But man lacks the desire for Christ and
    the things of God until God creates in his soul a positive
    inclination for these things."[xviii]

Can We Really Choose Sin or Righteousness?

To emphasize an important truth, I want to rephrase an earlier quote
from Sproul. When you make a decision, whether consciously or
unconsciously, it originates from your strongest desire. In other words,
each time you decide, it reveals what you find most satisfying or pleasurable at that moment.

At its core, Edwards argues that humanity cannot fulfill God's will
without His intervention and empowerment. Take a moment to
consider the implications of the following two verses as they relate to
Edwards' point.

Now may the God of peace—who brought up from the dead our Lord
Jesus, the great Shepherd of the sheep, and ratified an eternal covenant
with his blood— may he equip you with all you need for doing his will.
May he produce in you, through the power of Jesus Christ, every good
thing that is pleasing to him. All glory to him forever and ever! Amen.
Hebrews 13:20–21, NLT

Dear friends, you always followed my instructions when I was with
you. And now that I am away, it is even more critical. Work hard to
show the results of your salvation, obeying God with deep reverence

and fear. For God is working in you, giving you the desire and the power to do what pleases him.

PHILIPPIANS 2:12–13, NLT

To effectively address the question in my header, "Can I choose sin or righteousness?" I will use an illustration involving two tables, the table of sin and the table of righteousness. This illustration will reveal the truth of Augustine's prayer, "Oh God, grant what thou dost command and command what thou dost desire." Imagine entering a room with a large table, the table of sin, at its center. A sign on the wall states that you may choose as many items (all sinful) as you like from the table. You see many appealing items that could increase your pleasure, so you make several choices. As non-believers, we lived this way and made choices freely, but sometimes, upon reflection, we knew they never satisfied us for long. But what other options did we have? One thing remained: our greatest desire was rooted in our love of ourselves (fruit of the flesh, Galatians 5:19–21).

But one day, through God's great mercy (Titus 3:5) and grace (Ephesians 2:8–9), the gospel was shared with you by a neighbor you hadn't particularly liked, even though he was kind in some ways. He invited you for coffee, opened his Bible, and carefully explained the gospel to you. Although you had heard it before, this time you had a mysterious interest because the Holy Spirit opened your mind through regeneration, enabling you to understand the gospel in a way you never had before. The Holy Spirit illuminated your mind with the truth of God's Word and gave you the gift of faith (Ephesians 2:8–9), which you joyfully exercised authentically, confessing Jesus as your Lord and believing in your heart that God the Father raised Jesus (God the Son) from the dead (Romans 10:9–10), resulting in your eternal salvation. This marked the beginning of the freedom Jesus mentioned in John 8:31–32: "So Jesus was saying to those Jews who had believed Him, 'If you abide in My word, then you are truly My disciples; and you will know the truth, and the truth will make you free.'"

Previously, as a non-believer, you had no trust in God; however, trusting yourself seemed safe and reasonable. You had no interest in living righteously, so there was only one table you could choose from—the table of sin, filled with the fruit of the flesh (sexual immorality, impurity, sensuality, idolatry, sorcery, enmities, strife, jealousy, outbursts of anger, selfish ambition, dissensions, factions, envying, drunkenness, carousing, and things like these) (Galatians 5:19–21). But as a Christian, you now have more options: the table of sin, filled with sinful fruit, and the table of righteousness, filled with the fruit of the Spirit (love, joy, peace, patience, kindness, goodness, faithfulness, gentleness, and self-control; Galatians 5:22–23).

As a non-believer, you had no interest in any of the items on the table of righteousness and lacked the desire or inclination to choose any of them (Psalm 115:5–8; Hebrews 3:12–13). Nevertheless, you freely exercised your will by selecting many of the items on the table of sin. Your will functioned properly; your only limitation was that your greatest inclination was enslaved to sin and consumed by self-centeredness (Romans 3:10–18; Ephesians 2:1–3). Because you were permanently selfish, the items of sin were the only ones that brought you pleasure. Your will was free to act, but it was always limited to choosing from the table of sin.

But now that you are a Christian, the righteousness and holiness of Christ have been imputed to your life positionally (Romans 4:22–5:1, 17–19; 2 Corinthians 5:21; 2 Peter 1:4). This means you are now justified, standing in God's royal courtroom, declared not guilty, and, therefore, positionally holy. When you accepted Christ, your willpower didn't change, but since you are no longer enslaved to sin (Romans 6:6, 18) and are a new creation in Christ (2 Corinthians 5:17), you now have a hunger for the fruit of the Holy Spirit. Both tables are available for you to choose from. Yes, you have been freed from the enslavement to sin, but the presence of sin still remains within you. You now have the freedom to choose between the table of sin (fruit of the flesh) and the table of righteousness (fruit of the Spirit). The table of sin still offers all the choices it had before you became a Christian, but through your sanctification, those options are gradually becoming less appealing. Meanwhile, the table of righteousness, filled with choices that honor God, is becoming more desirable, and because of the Holy Spirit's work in you, His fruit will become your greatest inclination.

You have a strong desire to avoid sin and pursue the items on the table of righteousness. These righteous desires were absent before your conversion, but now they hold great importance for you. Oh yes, you can still see the table of sin and all its sinful options. Not only can you see these options, but you also have the freedom to choose any of them at any time (1 John 1:6–7, 2:10–11). Sometimes, you do pick from the table of sin, which then, due to the Holy Spirit's conviction, prompts you to confess (1 John 1:9); be quick to do this. However, even when tempted to choose from the table of sin, deep down, you wish that table didn't exist, and one day it won't (Revelation 21–22).

For the first time in your life, you become aware of "a battle in your mind"—a conflict between the table of sin and the table of righteousness. You are growing in hating the table of sin and the struggle; yet sometimes, you find yourself doing the very things you despise—choosing from the table of sin (Galatians 5:17), just like the apostle Paul (Romans 7:15). Day by day, moment by moment, you have the freedom to choose any items from either table whenever you wish. However, Paul teaches that victory in the battle between your mind (that which is eternal) and your flesh (that which is mortal and will be destroyed upon your death or the rapture) is found only in Jesus Christ, your Lord (Romans 7:24–25).

Since You Now Have the Freedom to Choose from Either Table, How Does Your Desire for the Table of Righteousness Grow?

When you were previously enslaved to sin, you didn't realize it because you were deceived by sin (Hebrews 3:12–13) and the devil (Revelation 12:9). The biggest problem with deception is that you don't know you're deceived. This has nothing to do with your Bible knowledge but everything to do with the nature of sin and the devil. If you were aware, you wouldn't be deceived. This principle underscores the importance of daily putting on the armor of God (Ephesians 6:10–18). Doing so helps you guard against deception as you wear the belt of truth (Ephesians 6:14) and wield the sword of the Spirit, the Word of God (Ephesians 6:17). As you continue to saturate your mind not only with the knowledge of Scripture but also with the intention to obey it by guarding your mind with it (Psalm 119:11), your deception will decrease, and Yahweh will become your greatest delight (Psalm 73:25). This intentional lifestyle results in your prayers aligning with His will and your greatest desires (inclinations) being fulfilled (Psalm 37:4; John 15:7). I will discuss in chapter three, when talking about renewing your mind, how your desires change.

But in the meantime, you understand that your choices have expanded—they now include sin and righteousness. Since you are no longer enslaved to sin and, as a child of light, you begin walking in the light (1 John 1:7), you have the freedom to choose your primary inclination, whether it is based on the sin within you or the love of Jesus (Colossians 3:17; 2 Corinthians 5:14; Romans 2:4; Hebrews 12:28–29; 2 Corinthians 3:18; Romans 15:13; Genesis 32:10; Psalm 94:18–19; Psalm 130:3–4). As you mature through sanctification, you increasingly desire to deny yourself, take up your cross, and follow Jesus (Luke 9:23; Galatians 2:20). Jesus wants you to understand and experience His love and kindness toward you, as revealed in His ongoing forgiveness of your sins (2 Corinthians 5:14; Romans 2:4). Your growth in practical holiness should be motivated not by fear of judgment or obligation to obey, but by your Savior's love and kindness toward you (1 John 4:16–19) and by your love for Him (John 14:21). It is Christ's love for you, combined with your love for Him, that draws you away from the attraction of sin and toward the righteousness and holiness of Christ.

We all reap what we sow. When you sow to sin, you will reap the fruit of the flesh recorded in Galatians 5:19–21. In these verses, you find many ungodly, negative actions and feelings that are the result of sin and the lies within you. This fruit comes from your choice to follow the inclinations of the flesh. But when your greater inclinations are of the Holy Spirit, His fruit (Galatians 5:22–23) will flow out of you in abundance, which includes many positive actions and feelings, all based on righteousness and truth.

Are You Driven or Drawn?

I want to conclude this chapter with two scenarios to help you identify which one best describes your life. One involves cattle, and the other involves sheep. If you've ever seen a cattle drive in person or on TV, you'll notice the cattle are driven from behind by cowboys, horses, and sometimes dogs. What emotions do the cattle feel? In other words, why are they running? I suggest they run out of fear of the cowboys, horses, and dogs. These three drivers have no relationship with the cattle and no desire for one. They aim to move the cattle through fear and coercion to a specific destination. The well-known Twenty-Third Psalm portrays Jesus as the perfect Shepherd who carefully cares for each member of His flock. Notice the differences between the Good Shepherd and the cattle drivers. Does the Shepherd force His sheep by staying behind them without forming a relationship? Or does He quietly draw them from the front, staying in their view so they can see, hear, and follow Him? He doesn't drive from behind using fear; instead, He draws them from the front through love. Fear and anxiety should have no place in a sheep's relationship with its Shepherd (Isaiah 41:10; Philippians 4:6–7). Instead, the Shepherd aims to foster a relationship of love, joy, and peace (1 John 3:1, 4:9–10; Ephesians 2:4–5) with each of His sheep.

The Shepherd maintains a relationship with each sheep and desires that it trusts and obeys His every gesture. His rod and staff guide and direct His sheep toward an eternal, glorious destination (Psalm 73:23–24). Instead of fleeing from the Shepherd, the sheep learn that He truly loves them, and they yearn for Him more than anything on earth (Psalm 73:25), drawing near to Him because of His everlasting love (Psalm 73:26). Because these sheep experience the Shepherd's love, they long to know Him intimately (Philippians 3:7–11) and therefore choose His path of truth (Galatians 5:25) over their own path of sin and lies. They choose to live by the Spirit and, as a result, do not carry out the deeds of their own flesh (Galatians 5:16).

Another way to understand living by the Spirit is to abide in Jesus (John 15:5). The believer who has a genuine desire to do good (Romans 7) still won't achieve this without abiding in Christ (John 15:5; Romans 8). The most a believer can do, apart from abiding in Christ (living by the Spirit, Galatians 5:16) or being filled with the Spirit (Ephesians 5:18), is to try to produce the fruit of the Spirit through human effort. This effort will not bring glory to God and will only be burned up like wood, hay, and straw (1 Corinthians 3:12–15). (To learn more about abiding in Christ, see my book *The Life I Want in Christ* on Amazon.)

Just as Augustine's prayer, "Oh God, grant what thou dost command and command what thou dost desire," expresses, these sheep desire to follow their Shepherd's commands but need His enablement to do so (Hebrews 13:20–21; Philippians 2:12–13). It is a crucial truth for all sheep to understand that to obey from the heart, self-denial and a close, abiding relationship with the Shepherd are necessary (John 15:5). In *The Valley of Vision* we read, "By reason I see a thing is so; by faith I know it as it is."[xix] Through faith, you not only possess knowledge but also conviction, which becomes evident when you choose to live in the truth rather than in your feelings.

Many empirical observations around us seem to contradict God's love and care for His children. However, as mentioned in Habakkuk 2:4

(also see Romans 1:17; Galatians 3:11; Hebrews 10:38), the righteous are not instructed to live by empirical observations but by faith. This means we choose to live by what we cannot yet see but lasts forever. Although it is difficult, you must not obsessively focus on your problems, even though they are real. Why? Because they will soon be gone (2 Corinthians 4:18).

Here on earth, the saints can exist in two separate worlds, but you can't be part of both at once—you must choose one to inhabit. The choice you make depends on your strongest inclination at that moment and will determine the outcome of your deepest desire. Christians must understand that selecting from the table of righteousness, regardless of feelings, is demonstrated by obeying God's Word, which shows your love for Christ (John 14:21).

Your walk-and-talk reveals what matters most to you right now. In Psalm 11:1b–3, David encounters two different voices speaking to him. His friends tell him to run to the mountains and hide, but deep inside, he knows he should find refuge in his Lord.

Living in freedom means not trying to follow God's law to earn righteousness, while avoiding a life controlled by feelings. In other words, true freedom is only possible when we choose to live in the truth. A life that trusts God in every big and small experience, regardless of emotional ties, is genuinely free. Choosing this way of life allows us to experience the freedom Jesus intends for us (Galatians 5:1). We can do nothing that glorifies the Father unless we abide in Jesus (John 15:5–8). Therefore, we cannot glorify God when we are in bondage to our feelings.

As I mentioned earlier, your will is always guided by what you find most pleasurable. When experiencing negative emotions, acknowledge that your Lord is sovereign over your circumstances, and ask Him to teach you the lessons He wants you to learn. Don't operate from your self-centered perspective; instead, choose to live in the truth by being God-centered. This will free you to pursue God's purposes, rather than being held back by negative feelings. In the movie *The Matrix*,[xx] the choice is between the red pill and the blue pill. If you choose the blue pill, you can believe whatever you want, remain ignorant of reality, and continue living a life of deception and bondage. But if you choose the red pill, which represents reality, you will experience freedom. In principle, this holds for Christians. If you select a life guided by feelings, you will live a life of deception and bondage. However, choosing to surrender to Jesus, who is the truth, will lead to the freedom that God intends for you. Which do you choose—the blue pill of deception or the red pill of truth?

The sin within you is drawn to the table of sin and will cease to exist at your death or the rapture. In Romans 7, the apostle Paul states that when he sins, the cause is not him (the new creation) but the sin within him. Your flesh, which houses your sin, is all that people will see in your casket. The real you will be with Christ in heaven forever (1 Corinthians 15:12–58). In the meantime, choose to avoid being enslaved by negative feelings. This doesn't mean you deny your feelings; rather, it means you avoid being ruled by them. This is done by knowing and choosing to live in the freedom of the promises of God, even when you don't feel that way. Remember, negative feelings are not the truth; they are feelings and will never set you free from the bondage they can hold you in. The only source of freedom is choosing to trust in God's presence, promises, and power, regardless of your feelings.

I encourage you to listen to the hymn "Trust and Obey" by John H. Sammis (1887).

Small-group Discussion Questions

1. Why is living by the Spirit essential for obeying the truth of Scripture?

2. How have you changed since becoming a follower of Jesus regarding your will?

3. As a Christian, how is your freedom greater in relation to the two tables?

Suggestions for Freedom of the Will

1. Remember, your greatest desire influences your will. Your desires are directly connected to what you believe (true or false) will bring you the most pleasure.

2. Negative emotions indicate something—it's not wrong to feel them, since often you have no conscious control over the negative feelings that quickly surface. However, the critical part is not the feelings themselves but whether you respond with the fruit of the Spirit. To do that, you need truth to be your greatest inclination. Since the Holy Spirit dwells within you and is writing God's Word on your heart, He can cause (Ezekiel 36:26–27) you to live in truth if you call to Him for help (Psalm 25:4–5). This will result in a life that is described in Psalm 119.

3. Don't try to create your own way to remove or alter negative feelings. Instead, realize that God is within you, and focus on connecting with Him in His peace and joy as you trust Him to give you victory.

Chapter Three

FREEDOM THROUGH A RENEWED MIND

I beseech you therefore, brethren, by the mercies of God, that you present your bodies a living sacrifice, holy, acceptable to God, which is your reasonable service. And do not be conformed to this world, but be transformed by the renewing of your mind, that you may prove what is that good and acceptable and perfect will of God.
ROMANS 12:1–2, NKJV

According to Romans 12:1–2, avoiding conformity to this world and living in the freedom Jesus has given requires a conviction to identify the false belief (lie) behind our sin. In Paul's teaching, he regularly moves from doctrine to practice. The more we grow in practical sanctification, the closer we come to perfected practical holiness (2 Corinthians 3:18). Our pursuit of practical holiness is supported by renewing our minds. A renewed mind requires not only recognizing wrong beliefs (lies) but also replacing them with the truth, as shown in living them out regardless of how we feel.

The following story was written by Corrie ten Boom and taken from the *Guideposts* classics website. It beautifully portrays both forgiveness and the process of renewing our minds.

Corrie and her sister Betsie were arrested in Holland for concealing Jews in their home during the Nazi occupation. They were imprisoned at the Ravensbrück concentration camp. There, both women, along with many others, were ridiculed and shamed by their captors. It was there that Betsie died. But that was all in the past. Now, after the war, Corrie had the privilege of teaching many of the Hollanders the necessity of forgiveness.

It was 1947, and I had come from Holland to defeated Germany with the message that God forgives. It was the truth they needed most to hear in that bitter, bombed-out land, and I gave them my favorite mental picture. Maybe because the sea is never far from a Hollander's mind, I liked to think that's where forgiven sins were thrown.

One evening, Corrie was teaching at a church in Munich, a city in southeastern Germany. During her message, Corrie said,

When we confess our sins, God casts them into the deepest ocean, gone forever. The solemn faces stared back at me, not quite daring to believe. There were never questions after a talk in Germany in 1947. People stood up in silence, collected their wraps in silence, and left the room in silence.

Corrie was preparing to leave the church when she looked up and saw a man not leaving but walking down the aisle toward her. He was overweight, wearing an overcoat and a brown hat. She thought there was something familiar about him, and then she recognized him, recalling his blue German uniform and visored cap with skull and crossbones. Seeing him took her back to a huge room with harsh overhead lights. She could see piles of women's clothing and piles of their shoes. Corrie, Betsie, and the rest of the imprisoned women had been forced to walk shamefully naked before this cruel captor.

He walked up to her, hand extended, and said, "A fine message, fräulein! How good it is to know that, as you say, all our sins are at the bottom of the sea!" She tried to avoid taking his hand by fumbling in her purse. She knew he didn't recognize her, but she remembered him! "It was the first time since my release that I had been face-to-face with one of my captors, and my blood seemed to freeze."

He said he had been a guard at the Ravensbrück concentration camp, where Corrie and Betsie had endured his brutality. He said he had become a Christian and, even though God had forgiven him, he asked Corrie for her forgiveness as he held out his hand. Corrie stood frozen, wondering whether to touch the man's hand, but how could she forgive him?

Here is what was going on in Corrie's mind:

And I stood there—I whose sins had every day to be forgiven—and could not. Betsie had died in that place—could he erase her slow terrible death simply for the asking?

It could not have been many seconds that he stood there, hand held out, but to me it seemed hours as I wrestled with the most difficult thing I had ever had to do.

For I had to do it—I knew that. The message that God forgives has a prior condition: that we forgive those who have injured us. "If you do not forgive men their trespasses," Jesus says, "neither will your Father in heaven forgive your trespasses."

And still I stood there with the coldness clutching my heart. But forgiveness is not an emotion—I knew that too. Forgiveness is an act of the will, and the will can function regardless of the temperature of the heart.

"Jesus, help me!" I prayed silently. "I can lift my hand. I can do that much. You supply the feeling."

And so woodenly, mechanically, I thrust my hand into the one stretched out to me. And as I did, an incredible thing took place. The current started in my shoulder, raced down my arm, sprang into our joined hands. And then this healing warmth seemed to flood my whole being, bringing tears to my eyes.

"I forgive you, brother!" I cried. "With all my heart!"

For a long moment we grasped each other's hands, the former guard and the former prisoner. I had never known God's love so intensely as I did then.[i]

Are We Renewing Our Minds?

A powerful and inspiring true story underscores the importance of living in truth rather than following feelings. As I read this story, I imagined Corrie's facial expressions and heard her internal cries as she responded to what God was instructing her to do. Corrie felt trapped by years of negative emotions and mental pain. It would have been so easy to choose from the table of sin to respond to her former captor. Why couldn't she give in to the offerings of the table of sin? Because, as a believer, Corrie was no longer blinded by the god of this age (2 Corinthians 4:4) or deceived by the sin in her (Hebrews 3:12).

For years, Corrie had read and studied God's Word. She was reminded of the truth reflected in Jesus' glorious life, as seen in the Gospels (2 Corinthians 3:18). As she stood before this man asking for her forgiveness, she was no longer enslaved to the table of sin. For Corrie, torn by painful, fiery emotions, the sinful options were real and very tempting. But, as with Augustine and the apostle Paul, Corrie recognized the right course of action and relied on Christ's help to choose what was right and true. Even though Corrie was not always conscious of the Holy Spirit's work, He had continued to renew her mind since her conversion (Titus 3:5). The Spirit guided her toward the love of Christ and His kindness, helping her avoid sin (2 Corinthians 5:14; Romans 2:4). Therefore, she chose to extend her hand and forgive her new brother. Living in the truth, with the Holy Spirit's help, moved her further along the path of freedom and practical holiness, making her more like Jesus in His glory and character (2 Corinthians 3:18).

Do you see the truth in this story of forgiveness that helped Corrie make the right choice? She remembered that God had forgiven and still forgives her for her many sins. Corrie also recalled that God's forgiveness is directly connected to her willingness to forgive others (Matthew 6:12). God responds to His children's sins in the same way we forgive or refuse to forgive others. Corrie understood these truths as commands in Scripture, as did Augustine in his prayer, "Oh God, grant what thou dost command and command what thou dost desire." She knew what God commanded, but she also realized she needed His help to obey. So, what did Corrie do? She identified three other truths: forgiveness is not an emotion, it is an act of the will, and the will can operate regardless of the heart's feelings.

Knowing what God commands and recognizing that she wanted to do it, she understood she needed and desired His help. Corrie's struggle was not physical but spiritual. It was a struggle to avoid the lies of negative feelings and to choose the truth of God's Word, which is part of renewing our minds. An important biblical activity that helps renew our minds is recorded in 2 Corinthians 10:3–5:

For though we walk in the flesh, we do not war according to the flesh, for the weapons of our warfare are not of the flesh, but divinely powerful for the tearing down of strongholds, as we tear down speculations and every lofty thing raised up against the knowledge of God, and take every thought captive to the obedience of Christ.

The context of the verses above is spiritual warfare, in which Paul was being accused by false teachers of immorality, corruption, greed, and pride. Regardless of the specifics of your warfare, each battle requires you to be well-equipped not only with patience and courage but also with the weapons of righteousness. Paul commends every Christian as a minister of God, to be "in the word of truth, in the power of God; by the weapons of righteousness for the right hand and the left" (see 2 Corinthians 6:4–7). All Christians are Christ's soldiers fighting a spiritual battle against the Enemy's false ideologies spread throughout the world. Non-believers are blinded and captivated by these false beliefs, and Christians can also be deceived if they don't know the truth of God's Word. Both groups can only be freed by understanding and living in the truth of Scripture. Spiritual warfare is a battle for the minds of non-believers, freeing them from the lies of the kingdom of darkness, and for Christians, replacing those lies with God's truth. This is what the battle is about and why renewing our minds is so necessary for daily victory. We are to fight for the truth of Scripture, the glory of Jesus, our practical holiness, and the salvation of sinners. Therefore, when we are aware of the battle between choosing from the table of sin or righteousness, it's important to note that this battle is not won by physical strength. As the apostle Paul points out in these verses, this is a spiritual battle that we are to take captive to God for help.

What Does It Mean to Take Our Thoughts Captive to the Obedience of Christ?

Slowly read the following verses from Proverbs 3:5–6 to gain an Old Testament perspective on this question: "Trust in Yahweh with all your heart, and do not lean on your own understanding. In all your ways acknowledge Him, And He will make your paths straight." Our focus is to trust Yahweh in what He says about how we are to live rather than in how we think we should live. This lifestyle is fostered by knowing God's

Word and by abandoning any intellectual independence that opposes Scripture. This practice deepens our relationship with Jesus (John 14:21). The word *acknowledge* (*yada*) means "to experience Yahweh relationally." It is a word of intimacy that conveys engaging Yahweh with all of our being, including submitting our personal thoughts and inclinations to Him with the intent of living the way He instructs us to live (Psalm 32:8), regardless of how we feel. This is how we take our thoughts captive to Christ, and this is how our sanctification is achieved (John 17:17). If we don't do this, our thoughts tend to take us captive, which is a form of bondage. But when we take our thoughts captive to Christ, we are in the process of being transformed by the renewing of our minds (Romans 12:2). This is a mind set on the Spirit, which leads to life and peace (Romans 8:5–6). It's important to recognize that the Enemy plants doubt, anxiety, and fear in our minds. Therefore, casting them on Jesus (1 Peter 5:7) helps renew our minds and helps us experience the freedom Jesus set us free to have (Galatians 5:1).

Corrie said she made a cold-blooded decision. Her strongest inclination was to forgive, which aligns with the truth of Scripture. Emotions are not evil unless they stem from sinful inclinations. If someone hurts us and we want revenge, unrighteous anger often follows. However, in her dealings with her new Christian brother, Corrie prayed and then chose to do what was right: forgive her former adversary. That choice led to Corrie's freedom.

When someone has conviction, she not only knows what to do but also acts on it, even when her feelings run counter to it. Corrie had the conviction to live in the truth. She knew the truth, wanted to live by it, and therefore sought God's help. She silently prayed, "Jesus, help me!" and Jesus helped her; her conviction was evident in her forgiveness of the German guard (a former enemy). Her forgiveness was grounded in truth, not emotion. She knew the truth that her sins were cast into the sea. Corrie chose to live in the Spirit and therefore didn't carry out the deeds of her flesh (Romans 8:5–10).

A Strategy of Satan

Years ago, I read a book by Warren W. Wiersbe titled *The Strategy of Satan*. In this concise yet deeply insightful book, Wiersbe describes the five *D*s of the devil: doubt, deceive, destroy, divide, and death. The first book of the Bible shows Satan as the deceiver (Genesis 3), and the last book depicts him as a deceiver (Revelation 12:9). In Genesis 3:1, Satan begins by planting doubt: "Has God said?" This is followed in Genesis 3:4, where the devil deceives Eve, saying, "You surely will not die!" Satan's next move is to destroy the validity of God's word in Eve's mind by making it seem trivial. Eve's misunderstanding becomes clear in Genesis 3:6: "Then the woman saw that the tree was good for food, and that it was a delight to the eyes, and that the tree was desirable to make one wise, so she took from its fruit and ate; and she also gave to her husband with her, and he ate." Eve's deception and the weakening of the authority of God's word in her mind naturally led to division, the fourth step in Satan's strategy. This division appears in four ways. First, there is division within themselves. Because of their sin, they felt fear (v. 10) for the first time, realizing they were naked (vv. 7, 10). They now held a distorted and sinful view of themselves because their identity was no longer rooted in the Father of Truth but in the Father of Lies. Second, driven by their fear and shame, they tried to hide from God, creating a division between them and their loving Father (v. 8). Third, when questioned about their sin, division arose between the once-perfect couple, with Adam blaming Eve (v. 12). Meanwhile, Eve blamed the serpent (v. 13). Neither was willing to accept personal responsibility. Further division appears in Eve's sinful desire to control her husband (v. 16) and Adam's desire to dominate his wife (v. 16). Fourth, a division between the first couple and creation is evident in Eve's pain during childbirth. At the same time, Adam's separation from creation shows in his pain and sweat as he works the land to eat (vv. 17–19). Having identified four examples of Satan's strategy of division—from within themselves, others, creation, and God—we now reach Satan's fifth and final strategy: death. In Genesis 2:16–17, the Creator of the universe warned Adam that eating from the forbidden tree would lead to death (physical and spiritual)—a complete separation from God. As we learned in chapter two of this book, the main point is that our strongest inclination governs our will.

In the story of Satan, Adam, and Eve, Satan's attack targeted the truth when he tried to deceive Eve, first tempting her to doubt God's truth. This is our greatest threat. The best way to avoid deception (Proverbs 14:12; Colossians 3:2) is not to study every form of deception but to become thoroughly familiar with God's truth and His love.

Then, when faced with falsehood, we will instantly recognize that it is not the truth.

The problem with trusting our own insights is that it feels so easy and natural. Jesus shares a parable about a rich man in Luke 12:16–17: "And He told them a parable, saying, 'The land of a rich man was very productive. And he began reasoning to himself, saying, What shall I do, since I have no place to store my crops?'" Notice with whom the man reasons—himself, not God. There is a serious problem when we rely on our own insights rather than trust God's truth. Proverbs 3:5–6 instructs us not to lean on our understanding. In other words, if we want to be a godly person, we should focus on God's truths rather than on ourselves, for the sin within us is deceptive (Hebrews 3:13). Deception always leads to bondage; truth always brings freedom. We choose which path to follow. That's why wearing the belt of truth (Ephesians 6:14) is so necessary to be victorious when tempted.

Renewing Our Minds with the Truth

Knowing and understanding God's Word is essential to the Christian life. But how often have we said or behaved in a way that we knew was wrong and did it anyway? Usually, we are quickly convicted by the Holy Spirit that our thoughts, words, or actions are sinful. Then we might remember 1 John 1:9 and immediately confess our sin, only to repeat the sin again and again. For many of us, this becomes a recurring pattern. How do we break it? Romans 12:1–2 instructs Christians to renew their minds. Our part in the renewing process requires more than knowledge and understanding of God's Word. It involves replacing the lies in our minds with the truth of Scripture. But be encouraged, the Holy Spirit is also renewing our minds, and He is graciously doing it every day (2 Corinthians 4:16).

Imagine you're playing basketball with some of your Christian neighbors. It's a fun and competitive game. At one point, you try to make a layup and are quickly hit in the face with the elbow of the person guarding you. You immediately turn to this person in anger, loudly yelling at him, and push him. Suddenly, the game falls silent, and everyone on the court is staring at you. Instantly, you realize in your heart that the way you spoke and acted was sinful. Therefore, looking at all the players, especially the person who accidentally elbowed you in the face, you say, "I was wrong for yelling and pushing you. Would you please forgive me?" The individual who elbowed you quickly forgives you and offers any needed first aid. Now, my question is, "Does your confession equal renewing your mind?" In other words, does simply admitting what you did was wrong and asking for forgiveness mean you are renewing your mind? I suggest it does not. Imagine that next Saturday you have another basketball game with the same group of neighbors. This time, you try a jump shot, and the defender attempts to block it, but accidentally hits you in the head. Instantly, out of anger, you turn to him and yell at him. However, you don't push him because you remember pushing someone last week, and it didn't go well. So, even though you don't push him, inwardly you punched him in the face. What's happening? Did you not learn your lesson a week earlier?

Confessing to yelling and pushing the individual was a good step, but you missed a significant opportunity to further renew your mind. Do you remember what we learned in chapter two about your will? You will always respond to your strongest desire or inclination at the moment. Many of our beliefs are based on lies rather than truth. Since sin is deceptive (Hebrews 3:12–13), how can it ever be replaced with truth? Apart from the Holy Spirit's intervention, the lie is never exposed.

True repentance means turning away from the lies we believe and choosing to live in the truth. However, if our lie is never identified, we won't turn away from it toward the truth. It's easier, quicker, and less painful to simply say you're sorry and ask for forgiveness, but you won't recognize the lie (inclination) at the root of your behavior. A simple apology is a form of manipulation, an excuse to avoid identifying the serious problem within you. To have your mind regularly renewed, you need to ask the Spirit for His wisdom (James 1:5, 3:17–18; 2 Corinthians 4:16).

Ask yourself, "What am I believing that led to the yelling and pushing?" No speech or behavior comes from you that isn't directly connected to your strongest inclination at that moment. That inclination (lie) doesn't just disappear but lurks in our subconscious, ready to surface unless the Word of God replaces it. We don't control all the ideas, thoughts, and temptations that come into our minds, but we can choose not to focus on them.

Identifying lies in our minds takes time, effort, and the conviction that living in the truth is necessary to grow in Christlikeness. We need to be honest with ourselves and with God. A good friend and Christian counselor, Dennis Hughes, suggests we ask ourselves the following question: "What truth do I need to focus on that will promote better thoughts, words, and actions the next time?"

Renewing our minds means reordering our loves from anything and anyone to Christ (2 Corinthians 5:14). Be mindful of our thoughts: Are they opposed to God's Word? Philippians 4:8 states, "Finally, brothers, whatever is true, whatever is dignified, whatever is right, whatever is pure, whatever is lovely, whatever is commendable, if there is any excellence and if anything worthy of praise, consider these things." Paul mentions feelings in verses 6–7 and 10, thoughts in verse 8, and actions in verse 9. But note that he began with truth in verse 8. Neil Anderson writes,

> You do not get rid of negative thoughts by trying not to think of them. You overcome them by choosing the truth and continuing to choose the truth until the negative thoughts are drowned out or completely replaced by the truth. You let the peace of Christ rule in your heart by letting the words of Christ richly dwell within you. If you want to experience the freedom that Christ purchased for you and have a peace of mind that surpasses all understanding, then choose to think only those thoughts that agree with the Word of God.[ii]

I encourage you to listen to the hymn "May the Mind of Christ" by
Kate Barclay Wilkinson (1925).

Small-group Discussion Questions

1. What do you think motivated Corrie ten Boom to extend her hand of forgiveness to her former captor?

2. After listing the five *D*s of the devil, what is the benefit of understanding them?

    a.

    b.

    c.

    d.

    e.

    Benefit:

3. How does confessing your sins and renewing your mind promote growth in holiness?

Suggestions for a Renewed Mind

1. Pray daily for a deep, abiding relationship with Jesus (John 15:5).

2. Throughout the day, whenever you realize you've sinned, confess your sin immediately, identify the lie (your strongest desire) behind it, and ask God to help you replace it with His truth.

3. Before going to bed, make it a habit to mentally review your thoughts and events from the day, and ask the Lord to reveal any thoughts, words, or actions that dishonored Him. If something comes to mind, confess it, and then ask the Lord to show you the falsehood behind that sin and then replace it with God's truth (e.g., This is the lie I believed________, but this is the truth of God's Word________).

SUMMARY OF PART I: BIBLICAL FOUNDATIONS FOR OUR FREEDOM

(What God Has Done for You)

1. You are now positionally holy.

2. Your practical holiness is progressive and guaranteed.

3. The Holy Spirit empowers you to choose to live in truth.

4. Growth in freedom requires renewing your mind by replacing the lies in your mind with the truth of God's Word.

Now that we have examined the doctrinal truths (foundation) of chapters one through three regarding freedom, we turn to the remaining seven chapters, which will focus on applying these truths. However, I want to clarify one important point. In each chapter, I will focus on one feeling that everyone can experience. My goal is not to say, "Stop that, don't feel that way," because there is a better way. Instead, the issue isn't denying the feelings or giving up, but exploring your options. For example, if you walk out to your vehicle and see a flat tire, you don't pretend it's not flat and try to drive away. It's essential to accept that you have a flat tire and then consider the best way to glorify God in your response.

Rather than deny the truth of your flat tire, you could call AAA or a local mechanic, or you could get your car jack and replace the flat with a spare. Your goal is to identify which biblical truth relates to the chapter's topic and how you can live in that truth.

BIBLICAL LIVING FOR OUR FREEDOM

While section one (chapters one through three) provided the foundational truths for this book, section two (chapters four through ten) describes the practical application of those truths in daily life.

Chapter Four

FREEDOM FROM GUILT

For all have sinned; all fall short of God's glorious standard. Yet now God in his gracious kindness declares us not guilty. He has done this through Christ Jesus, who has freed us by taking away our sins. For God sent Jesus to take the punishment for our sins and to satisfy God's anger against us. We are made right with God when we believe that Jesus shed his blood, sacrificing his life for us. God was being entirely fair and just when he did not punish those who sinned in former times. And he is entirely fair and just in this present time when he declares sinners to be right in his sight because they believe in Jesus. Can we boast, then, that we have done anything to be accepted by God? No, because our acquittal is not based on our good deeds. It is based on our faith. So we are made right with God through faith and not by obeying the law.
ROMANS 3:23–28, NLT

You pulled into your driveway in your new car. It was shiny and gleaming in the sunlight. You left it in the driveway overnight, confident it would stay untouched thanks to your advanced security system. I lived in your neighborhood, and I not only saw your new car but also felt envious of it. I had a twenty-year-old car that needed a new transmission. I'm a mechanic, but I couldn't afford to fix it, so I drove it around town in third gear. Knowing about car security systems, I decided to put my skills to use. That night, I broke into your car, hotwired it, and drove away with your new vehicle—thank you very much! But there was one problem. I didn't realize your high-tech house security system was hidden and fully active. Later that night, two police officers knocked on my door and asked me to open my garage. I won't go into all the details, but I spent that night in jail. It wasn't long before I appeared before a judge, who carefully reviewed footage from your fancy security cameras showing me stealing your car. I was found guilty and sentenced to ten years in prison.

Ten years later, I was released. As I drove home in my thirty-year-old car, which still needed a transmission, I saw a welcome sight—a Dunkin' Donuts! I hadn't had their coffee in ten years. So, I turned on my turn signal (I'm not going back to jail!) and parked in the lot. I went inside and froze when I saw two police officers I recognized in the second booth. They were the same officers who had arrested me, taken me to jail, and testified against me about the car I stole. I felt embarrassed but knew it wasn't against the law to drink coffee and eat a donut. I sat with my back to the officers, savoring my coffee. However, as I sat there, I began to feel guilty about the car theft from ten years earlier. After a few minutes, I was tapped on the shoulder, and when I looked up, both offi-cers were standing in front of me. One said, "We recognize you, sir. You're the man who stole your neighbor's car about ten years ago." I shamefully replied, "Yes, sir, that was me." Suddenly, they grabbed me, pushed me against the table (spilling my coffee), and handcuffed me. I asked, "What are you doing? I was just drinking coffee." They said, "You are guilty of stealing your neighbor's car ten years ago. Off to court you go!"

Early the next morning, I was led into the courthouse with my wrists cuffed. When I entered, I saw you sitting there with a big smile on your face. The officers seated me, without an attorney, before the judge. The judge asked them why I had been brought into his courtroom. They said, "Your Honor, this man stole his neighbor's car ten years ago." Then you, my neighbor, stood up, pointed your finger at me, and said, "That's right, Your Honor, that guy is guilty of stealing my car!" Now, I ask you, the reader: Am I guilty of stealing my neighbor's car? Please understand, my question isn't whether I stole the car, but whether I am guilty of having stolen it. To answer this question correctly, I need to briefly define six legal terms: *evidence, judge, guilt, verdict, justice,* and *freedom.*

1. Evidence includes facts and information used to confirm or disprove whether a statement or event is true.

2. A judge is the legal official responsible for examining evidence and determining whether the law has been broken. If the law is violated, the judge issues a guilty verdict and sentences the offender in accordance with the legal requirements for the specific crime. However, if the evidence shows that the accused did not commit the crime, the judge will enter a verdict of not guilty. The accused is then released and free from any future charges arising from the original charge.

3. Guilt is a fact, not a feeling, that indicates someone has committed a specific crime or offense.

4. A verdict is the decision made by the judge or jury on whether a crime has been committed.

5. Justice is based on what is legally or morally right. If a judge determines the defendant is guilty, a sentence is imposed. If the judge decides the defendant is not guilty, the defendant is released.

6. Freedom is the power to think, speak, or act in any way you want without interference.

Now that these terms are defined, let's revisit the crime scene. At the scene, the police examined a clear and detailed digital recording of me stealing the car, including the date and time of the incident. After the judge carefully reviewed the digital recording, he issued a guilty verdict. To ensure justice, he sentenced me to ten years in prison. After serving my ten-year sentence, I was released and able to drink Dunkin' Donuts coffee whenever I wanted.

Therefore, am I guilty of stealing my neighbor's car? Well, as I stood before the judge, accused by the two police officers and my neighbor of being guilty of stealing the car, the judge asked if I had anything to say before he announced his verdict. I replied, "Your Honor, ten years ago, I did steal my neighbor's car and was brought before you for your verdict.

You found me guilty and sentenced me to ten years in prison. I have a letter in my pocket, written and signed by the warden of the state penitentiary, verifying that I served my ten-year sentence in full." After reviewing the letter and confirming its authenticity, the judge looked at me and delivered his decision. "Because you have satisfied my original sentence, you stand in my courtroom innocent of the charge of car theft, and therefore, I declare you not guilty. You are free to go."

When the judge declared me not guilty, I understood what he said, but deep down, I still felt guilty. While my head remained lowered to the floor, I said, "Your Honor, I don't know what to do because I still *feel* guilty." The judge very kindly and tenderly said to me, "Sir, your crime has been paid for in full. That is a fact; it is the truth. As your judge, I made my decision based on the truth of the evidence, never on feelings. For me to find you guilty based on feelings would be an injustice—I am a just judge. Therefore, I want you to leave my courtroom with your head held high, with peace and joy in your heart, for you stand righteous and innocent in my courtroom—not based on your feelings or mine, but on my declaration of the truth that you are not guilty. Next case!"

In my fictional story about stealing a car, I felt guilty. According to Romans 3:19 and 23, every person is guilty of sin and will be held accountable by God. This accountability is based on factual disobedience to God's Word, not on whether you feel you obeyed or disobeyed God. To clarify the truth that all Christians have been declared not guilty in Yahweh's royal courtroom, I want to explain five truths related to this critical topic.

First Truth: God Declares You Not Guilty!

Yet, now God in his gracious kindness declares us not guilty.
ROMANS 3:24a, NLT

God, the royal Judge of the universe, has declared all Christians not guilty (Romans 3:24). Guilt concerns your sinful thoughts, motives, and behaviors. In the New Testament, guilt is never a feeling; it is a legal, forensic term. It is grounded in truth, facts, and evidence. When Christians sin, the feeling they experience is not guilt but the conviction of the Holy Spirit. The Holy Spirit reveals your sin by reproving and convincing you of it (John 16:8). His purpose is that you confess your sins and experience the washing and renewal that come through Christ (1 John 1:9). When you confess your sin, God promises He will forgive you and cleanse you from all unrighteousness. This is a truth grounded in God's mercy, faithfulness, and righteousness, not in how you feel after confessing (1 John 1:9; Lamentations 3:22–23).

False guilt is common among Christians. It is a feeling, not a fact, that you've done something wrong, even when you haven't (e.g., when I felt guilty before the judge, even though he declared me not guilty). Sources of false guilt can include Satan (the accuser), false teaching, or a misunderstanding of Scripture. The necessary correction is to understand what Scripture truly teaches about your justification in Christ alone and to live in the freedom of this truth.

Another important legal term to understand is double jeopardy. In the 1999 crime thriller movie *Double Jeopardy*, which stars Ashley Judd, Tommy Lee Jones, Bruce Greenwood, and Annabeth Gish, Libby Parsons (Judd) is in prison for killing her husband, a crime she didn't commit. While in prison, she learns that her husband is still alive, faked his death, and left her to take the fall for it. A fellow inmate gives her bad legal advice, saying that since she has been convicted of killing her husband, she can find him after serving her sentence, kill him, and the State can't do anything to her because she has already served time for that crime. This is a misunderstanding of the double jeopardy principle. The law prevents someone from being tried twice for the same crime, but the movie does not depict that. In the film, if, after Libby Parsons is released from prison, she kills her husband, that act would not be covered by double jeopardy. Even though the same person is killed, it wouldn't be the same murder that got her locked up initially. It would be a different murder, in a different place, and at a different time. Since it wasn't the same offense, it would not qualify as double jeopardy.

Because of Jesus' perfect righteousness and His willingness to pay for all your sins—past, present, and future—and God the Father's willingness to accept Jesus' crucifixion on your behalf as a just and full payment, you can never be judged for any of your sins. Since Jesus paid the specific penalty for every sin you committed, you stand not guilty in God's royal courtroom. Therefore, to think or feel that God believes you guilty would be to believe a lie about God, for the Royal Judge of the universe cannot be unjust. Therefore, based on Jesus' work, not yours or your feelings, the judge has declared you not guilty.

In my story about stealing my neighbor's car, the judge declared me not guilty because I paid the penalty for my crime; therefore, my feelings were irrelevant and did not influence the judge's decision. The judge's justice was demonstrated when he enforced the penalty for breaking the law, and it was clear when he accepted my payment for my crime. This is similar to the Royal Judge's declaration that you are not guilty. No matter who accuses you—Satan, your neighbor, family, relatives, or even your conscience—based on Jesus' perfect sacrifice (payment), God, the Royal Judge of the Universe, has declared you not guilty. Your feelings cannot change the judge's decision. Next case!

Second Truth: All of Your Sins Have Been Taken Away.

He has done this (declared us not guilty) through Christ Jesus, who has freed us by taking away our sins.
Romans 3:24b, NLT

God completely cleared your criminal record by transferring all your sins (past, present, and future) to Jesus on the cross, and all of Jesus' righteousness in perfectly keeping God's law was transferred to your account. Jesus, being sinless and carrying all the sins of the elect, became sin so you could have eternal life. This truth is recorded in 2 Corinthians 5:21: "He made Him who knew no sin to be sin on our behalf, so that we might become the righteousness of God in Him." "If there is no sin, there is no guilt and therefore no condemnation" (Romans 8:1).

In the second truth statement, we encounter the encouraging truth of expiation. Expiation is a theological concept that includes forgiveness (1 John 1:9), purification (Psalm 51:7), and cleansing (Isaiah 1:18; Hebrews 10:17). This is illustrated in Psalm 103:12, where the psalmist states, "As far as the east is from the west, so far has He removed our transgressions from us." If you travel straight north and reach the North Pole, you will then begin heading south. Similarly, when reaching the South Pole, you will start heading north. However, a different principle applies when going east and west, which highlights Jesus' removal of your sins. If you travel west and continue until you return to your starting point, you will still be heading west, never east. That is expiation; that is how far God has removed your sins from you. God not remembering your sins reflects a relational promise (Romans 8:1).

Third Truth: Jesus Paid for All the Punishment of Christians.

For God sent Jesus to take the punishment for our sins and to satisfy God's anger against us.
Romans 3:25a, NLT

In the first truth statement, we learn that God has declared all Christians not guilty. The second truth teaches that all your sins have been removed and will never return. In the third truth, we find that Jesus paid for all your punishment. Propitiation is the making of reconciliation for one's sins (Hebrews 2:17). In other words, Jesus' crucifixion fully satisfied God's wrath against you (1 John 2:2; 4:10). Jesus has set you free, and it is a reality, regardless of how you feel.

The only kind of substitute that can satisfy God's wrath against each Christian must be a sinless man who willingly takes your place and is allowed by the Judge. There is only one who qualifies: Jesus, the God-Man. Therefore, when you fear that God will judge you for your sin, find comfort in 1 John 4:16–18, NLT:

> We know how much God loves us, and we have put our trust in his love. God is love, and all who live in love live in God, and God lives in them. And as we live in God, our love becomes more complete. So we will not be afraid on the day of judgment, but we can face Him with confidence because we live like Jesus here in this world. Such love has no fear, because perfect love drives out all fear. If we are afraid, it's because of the fear of punishment, and this shows that we have not fully experienced His perfect love.

The more you grow in experiencing God's love, the greater the peace and security you will experience on this side of heaven. Therefore, enjoy your freedom by choosing to rest in the truth that the royal Judge of the universe is eternally satisfied with the work His Son did for you on the cross.

Fourth Truth: You Are Made Right with God When You Believe.

We are made right with God when we believe that Jesus shed his blood, sacrificing his life for us...He declares sinners to be right in his sight because they believe in Jesus.
Romans 3:25b, 26b, NLT

Your guilty feelings are irrelevant. The Judge has already made His decision—not guilty! When you believe in your heart (Romans 10:9) that what Jesus did on the cross is acceptable to the royal Judge on your behalf, the Judge imputes all your sins to Jesus (Isaiah 53:4–5; 1 Peter 2:24) and transfers Jesus' righteousness to you (Romans 5:19; 1 Corinthians 1:30; 2 Corinthians 5:21; Philippians 3:9), regardless of how you feel. Therefore, you have been made right before God and stand justified in his courtroom. To fear God's judgment or to think you're guilty is to believe a lie. When you do this, Satan is pleased and feeds your fear and false beliefs. "Be subject therefore to God. Resist the devil, and he will flee from you" (James 4:7).

Fifth Truth: Live by Faith, Not by Works.

Can we boast, then, that we have done anything to be accepted by God? No, because our acquittal is not based on our good deeds. It is based on our faith.
Romans 3:27, NLT

There is no boasting in God's courtroom. The only kind of legitimate boasting you, as a Christian, can do is the kind described in Jeremiah 9:23–24:

Thus says Yahweh, "Let not a wise man boast in his wisdom, and let not the mighty man boast in his might; let not a rich man boast in his riches, but let him who boasts boast in this, that he understands and knows Me, that I am Yahweh who shows lovingkindness, justice, and righteousness on earth; for I delight in these things," declares Yahweh.

The truth in this passage is that Christians have nothing to boast about in their own abilities or behavior. The boasting that Jeremiah advocates is not self-centered but God-centered. It replaces all human pride with humility, gratitude, and loving obedience. Your acquittal is based on what Jesus did. It's not about what you do or don't do. I'm not saying you don't sin, but when you do, Jesus has already paid for that sin, and it is removed from your record—that's why you are not guilty.

When you feel sinful and guilty, you are not living by faith but by works. Remember, you have died to self and to sin (Galatians 2:20), and you are to live in and for the righteousness you received from Jesus at the moment you believed in your heart that God raised Jesus from the dead. This requires choosing to break free from the bondage of your changing feelings and to accept the freedom the royal Judge has granted you.

Positionally, God placed every Christian in Christ, who satisfied the law on the cross for your sins and guilt. Therefore, the law has no claim on you, because you are "in Christ" and are not a sinner but a saint (a new creature in Christ, 2 Corinthians 5:17).

Authentic faith is demonstrated by someone who lives out the truth that Jesus' death, burial, and resurrection are enough to satisfy the royal Judge. This is what Jesus meant when He said, "It is finished!" Wolgemuth and Tada offer a fitting conclusion to this chapter: "Undeniable guilt, plus undeserved grace, should equal unbridled gratitude."[i]

A great song to listen to is "What Sin" by Morgan Cryar (1997).

Small-group Discussion Questions

1. What is the greatest personal benefit in knowing that, according to God's declaration, you will never be condemned?

2. How would you explain to someone that God's justice and mercy are both demonstrated at the cross, based on God's declaration that you are not guilty?

3. Choose one of the five truth statements and describe how you can better live it out in your life.

Suggestions for Freedom from Guilt

1. Remember, there is no double jeopardy; you will never be punished for any sins you have committed, are committing, or will commit.

2. Remember, guilt is not a feeling!

3. Remember, the devil, others, or your own conscience are not your judges. Your loving, heavenly Father is the supreme Judge of the universe and has declared you not guilty.

Chapter Five

FREEDOM FROM WORRY

Be anxious for nothing, but in everything by prayer and petition with thanksgiving let your requests be made known to God. And the peace of God, which surpasses all comprehension, will guard your hearts and your minds in Christ Jesus.
Philippians 4:6–7

Imagine what it would be like not to worry at all. How would your life change if you had no worries? Is living a worry-free life even possible? It is possible, but as you might guess, it's directly connected to living in the truth.

Tom and Ruth just hit the road after spending a week with Tom's parents. They had enjoyed their time together and were now looking forward to a quiet five-hour drive home. Not long after leaving the town limits, they saw an emergency vehicle speed past them in the opposite direction. Both Tom and Ruth prayed for the safety and skill of the responders helping those in need. Within two minutes, Tom's cell phone rang—his mother calling to tell him that his dad had just suffered a heart attack. Tom's calm demeanor quickly gave way to considerable worry about his father's life. They immediately turned around and headed back to Tom's parents' house. As they pulled into his parents' driveway, the responders who had passed them were wheeling Tom's dad to the ambulance.

Let's pause to reflect on what happened. Were Tom and Ruth worried about Tom's dad before the emergency vehicle passed by them? Of course not; they had no idea of the true circumstances that had occurred thirty minutes earlier. They were peacefully looking forward to their trip home. But once they learned the truth—the reality at Tom's parents' house—they became worried and rushed back to help. Tom's dad had suffered a heart attack thirty minutes earlier while Tom and Ruth were quietly heading home. So, it wasn't that the heart attack had happened thirty minutes earlier, but that they were unaware of the true family circumstances. The point I'm making is that our response to events in our lives is directly linked to our perspective of them. Tom and Ruth prayed that the emergency responders could help the person in need, but they were completely unaware that it was Tom's dad. The circumstances stayed the same, but Tom and Ruth's understanding of the events changed. The key is knowing the truth of what is happening.

Before a worrying event in your life occurs, your decision to worry is closely tied to your strongest inclination. If the Lord Jesus were visiting Tom's parents when Tom's dad had a heart attack, do you think Tom and Ruth's reaction would have been different? Why? Because God is all-powerful, all-knowing, and present with Tom's dad, and He is good and always does what is best. So, what does Tom need to worry about? Tom might say, "Well, Jesus wasn't present with my parents," but is that really true? If Jesus is omnipresent, then Jesus was with Tom's dad. Even if Jesus wasn't physically with Tom's dad, isn't He still there spiritually, and isn't He omnipotent and omniscient?

My aim isn't to say you shouldn't worry about a family member having a heart attack. Instead, it's to help you understand that your emotions are directly tied to what you believe is true. If you don't recognize and accept that your emotions are linked to your current beliefs and inclinations, you'll never find a way to avoid being controlled by negative emotions. But how can you tell yourself not to worry about your dad as you see him being wheeled out of the house on a gurney? You can't tell yourself anything that will help you respond in a God-honoring way unless you rehearse God's truth in your mind. This family situation is part of God's sovereignty and the Spirit's sanctifying work in your life. The only way to grow in practical holiness is to live in the truth of God's Word, regardless of your circumstances.

On the Thursday night before Jesus was crucified, His love and concern for His disciples were perfect. He knew that the more He taught His disciples about His coming death, the more they would worry. Jesus wanted these men and us to give Him our worries (1 Peter 5:7; Psalm 55:22). Jesus was teaching His yoke (His truths) to His disciples and all Christians, for in Jesus' yoke we find rest (Matthew 11:29) from the worries of the world.

You find no lasting peace in feelings. In Matthew 6:31, Jesus said, "Do not worry then, saying, 'What will we eat?' or 'What will we drink?' or 'What will we wear for clothing?'" Furthermore, Jesus told His disciples not to worry about their lives since by worrying they couldn't even add a cubit to their lifespans (Luke 12:22, 25). It is foolish to worry about things you cannot change—a poor use of time. But you can choose to live in the truth Jesus proclaims about your life. You do this by trusting not your feelings but by abiding (resting, remaining) in what Jesus has already done for you (John 15:1–11). John MacArthur clearly states, "Worry, then, is a forbidden sin. And Jesus forbids it because it is incompatible with your Father, it is incompatible with your faith, and it is incompatible with your future. You are guaranteed by the grace of God a glorious future; is that not true?" [i]

On Thursday night, before Jesus was crucified, He taught His disciples, as recorded in John 13–17. The truth in these five chapters would be enough to help these eleven men get through the greatest loss of their lives. John 17 is often called Jesus' High Priestly Prayer. The disciples overheard Jesus' conversation with His heavenly Father. Jesus spoke not only to His Father about the eleven apostles but also about all present and future Christians on earth. That includes you. In John 17:17, we read that Jesus said God's Word helps us grow in our sanctification (not our feelings). You see, it is the truth of God that must replace our worries.

When you feel anxiety, fear, or similar emotions, you're not walking by the Spirit at that moment. Instead, you're relying on yourself, which is why you feel anxious or fearful. You're facing a situation beyond your control and abilities. This idea is easy to understand when you're not feeling anxious or fearful, but what do you do when you suddenly realize you're overwhelmed by a negative emotion? Remember, you became a Christian by hearing, understanding, and choosing to obey the truth. Christian growth follows the same pattern when dealing with negative feelings.

Steve Street, my good friend and a Christian counselor, shares the following helpful insights about walking in the truth:

In my practice, I talk with people a lot about "What If" thoughts, which are future-oriented, fearful thoughts: What if I get sick? What if I lose my job? What if . . .? I encourage people to fight "What If" thoughts with "What Is" thoughts: What Is true right now, What Is happening right now, What Is known right now. I also talk with people about how anxiety often comes from trying to control the future, which is impossible (Matthew 6:34).

Cognitive Behavior Therapy (CBT) teaches that one's thoughts drive one's emotions, which then drive one's behavior. I put this in terms of 3 H's for my clients: Head, Heart, Hand. First, you think (believe, Head), then you feel (Heart), then you act (Hand). I do think it is worth mentioning that sometimes anxiety is not fully one's choice (or an error in belief or thought), such as when one has a physiological condition contributing to anxiety, or when one suffers from PTSD or other trauma. It would be unhelpful, and possibly harmful, to tell someone who is experiencing a physiological condition that results in anxiety or when someone is reacting to unresolved trauma that they are in sin.

We read in Psalm 94:19, "When my anxious thoughts multiply within me, Your consolations delight my soul." Here, the psalmist teaches that God's comfort comes from His Word. We are challenged by the sufficiency of God's Word in Job 15:11–12a (NLT): "Is God's comfort too little for you? Is his gentle word not enough? What has taken away your reason?" Worry can fixate you on emotion and prevent you from seeing the truth. Worry is like playing catch with someone. Sometimes, the ball (worry) goes south, and other times it goes north. You become what is described in James 1:8: "being a double-minded man, unstable in all his ways." Worry essentially tells us to stop thinking and start feeling. The problem with this approach is that you will never discover the truth, and therefore, you cannot live in it. The prophet Isaiah offers us a choice in 26:3–4: "The steadfast of mind You will keep in perfect peace because he trusts in You. Trust in Yahweh forever, for in Yah—Yahweh Himself—we have an everlasting Rock."

The Devil's Five *D*s Revisited

Remember the *D*s of the devil? Worry causes you to doubt God's plan for your life by deceiving you; it destroys the credibility of God's Word in your mind. You are warned in Mark 4:19: "But the worries of the world, and the deceitfulness of riches, and the desires for anything else enter in and choke the word, and it becomes unfruitful."

In Matthew 13:22, we read, "And the one on whom seed was sown among the thorns is the person who hears the word, but the worries of the world and the deceitfulness of wealth choke the word, making it unfruitful." Here, we see worry (a close relative of anxiety) and deceitfulness working together to hinder God's Word. Usually, worry is about the future, but you know, you can't change the future, so why worry? Your focus should be on your Lord in the present. Max Lucado tells us, "Fear sees a threat. Anxiety imagines one."[ii]

I'll talk about fear in chapter seven, but I appreciate the distinction June Hunt makes between fear and worry: "Fear is an emotional reaction to a perceived, present danger. Whereas worry is mental distress over a possible, undesired happening in the future."[iii] The true way to handle either fear or worry is found in Psalm 50:15: "Call upon Me in the day of distress; I shall rescue you, and you will glorify Me."

Biblically, worry is a choice rooted in what you believe (remember the chapter on the will—we always choose from our greatest inclination). When you worry, you can always choose to pray or open your Bible and read hopeful passages (Deuteronomy 33:12; Joshua 1:9; Jeremiah 17:7; Psalm 3:1–8, 4:8, 13:2–5, 28:7, 34:4, 54:4, 86:7, 91:1–2, 109:21–22; Matthew 6:34; Luke 21:34; Philippians 4:6–7; Romans 15:13; 1 Peter 5:7). This helps redirect your mind away from playing catch with worry and sets you on the path of truth, which leads to growth in personal holiness. Usually, when I feel worried, it's because of my sin or someone else's. We are instructed to confess our sins (1 John 1:9) when we sin. When others sin against us, we are directed to forgive them (Ephesians 4:32). However, worry often arises when I doubt God's ability or willingness to handle the source of my concern. Another reason we worry is unbelief. I greatly appreciate the father's honesty in Mark 9:17–27 about his mute and deaf son, who was possessed by a demon. The father knew he didn't have the faith Jesus wanted ("if you can"), but he did have a little faith. A small amount of faith is better than none at all. If your faith is small, be encouraged:

according to Matthew 17:20, if your faith is the size of a mustard seed, it can move mountains!

God isn't looking for perfect faith, but He does want you to grow in faith—faith enough to pick up your sword of truth and experience freedom (John 8:31–32) by fighting against the lies in your mind. This is something you can do with God's help. Remember, the Lord wanted the father to have more faith, but the father knew his faith was small. So, what did he do? He asked Jesus to help him have more faith in Jesus. You can ask Jesus to do the same for you.

As I mentioned in the introduction, God hates all forms of bondage involving His children. Keep this truth in mind, as recorded in Romans 6:16 (NLT): "Don't you realize that you become the slave of whatever you choose to obey? You can be a slave to sin, which leads to death, or you can choose to obey God, which leads to righteous living." The choice is yours. Your mind will be renewed as you identify the lies in your mind related to worry and replace them with the truth of what your heavenly Father declares about His care for you.

God created you to find your worth and value in Him alone. This happens when you believe that God made you for Himself (Colossians 1:16). Being loved by Him and loving Him in return (Matthew 22:36–39) is the source of your significance (Psalm 57:2) and your security (Proverbs 14:26). Anxiety can't bring happiness, but trusting in what Jesus has done and will do for you can bring both present and eternal joy and peace (Romans 15:13).

Henri Nouwen wisely said, "Joy does not simply happen to us. We have to choose joy and keep choosing it every day. It is a choice based on the knowledge that we belong to God and have found in God our refuge and our safety and that nothing, not even death, can take God away from us."[iv]

Right and Wrong Experiences

In his book *Right Thinking*, Bill Hull writes,

> What scares me is the anti-intellectual, anti-critical-thinking philosophy that has spilled over into the Church. This philosophy tends to romanticize the faith, making the local church into an experience center . . .

Their concept of "church" is that they are spiritual consumers and that the church's job is to meet their felt needs.[v]

John Stott also warns about the dangers of living by your feelings: "Indeed, sin has more dangerous effects on our faculty of feeling than on our faculty of thinking, because our opinions are more easily checked and regulated by revealed truth than our experiences.[vi]

Experience isn't necessarily wrong; it depends on what you're going through. In Philippians 3:7–11, the apostle Paul seeks to know Christ through experience. He desires ongoing intimacy with his Savior, who is the Truth. John 8:31–32 calls us to know the truth through experience. When you obey the truth, you experience the freedom of obedience. Jesus is not suggesting that you only know facts about Scripture (see 1 Corinthians 8:1), but that you develop a living intimacy with Jesus, the source of all truth. Experiencing truth in this way differs significantly from focusing on your felt needs or feelings. Focusing on these can keep you in bondage and hinder your ability to experience ongoing intimacy with Jesus. According to Jesus, without this kind of experience (abiding), you can't glorify the Father (John 15:1–11). Focusing on felt needs is self-centered, while focusing on Christ is about loving and delighting in Him. Ask yourself, what is my strongest inclination? The choice is yours.

Another way to think about a life rooted in truth is to view truth as evidence. Many years ago, Josh McDowell wrote a helpful classic on apologetics. Years later, Josh and his son, Sean, revised and updated the book for a new generation. The book is titled *Evidence That Demands a Verdict*, with a subtitle of *Life-Changing Truth for a Skeptical World*. I am not aware of any rebuttal to this book, but if a counterargument does emerge, I might suggest the following title: *Feelings That Demand a Response: Life-Changing Felt Needs for an Emotionally-Driven Generation*. Maybe, maybe not? Living a life of faith requires a reasoned response to your current circumstances, grounded in the truth of God's Word. There's no other choice for a follower of Jesus.

Warrior Readiness

In chapter three, we learned that we should not think like the world; instead, we are to avoid conforming to its way of thinking. This requires an ongoing lifestyle of renewing your mind, which involves recognizing the lies you believe and replacing them with God's truth (Romans 12:2; Ephesians 4:23). This calls for deliberate warrior readiness by preparing your mind for action, as commanded in 1 Peter 1:13–16. Renewing your mind means stopping the habit of focusing on your circumstances and instead lifting your eyes to the truth of what lasts forever (Colossians 3:2; 2 Corinthians 4:18). The warrior of God raises his mighty shield of faith and skillfully wields the sword of the Spirit, which is the Word of God.

Worry indicates that you are relying on your own strength and focusing on your flesh to handle your circumstances. However, it shows you're not succeeding—you're worrying. The apostle Paul teaches that we need to shift from our limited abilities to the infinite power of the Holy Spirit (Romans 8:6). Worry is a fruit of the flesh, while peace is a fruit of the Spirit. My friend Dennis Hughes poses a very practical question: "Who would choose rotten worry over pleasant peace fruit?" He goes on to say that "an earthly focus that discounts a heavenly focus will result in holding the rotten fruit of worry. The fruit of peace comes when we fix our gaze on God and the hope of heaven."

You have been redeemed by the King of the universe, who gave you the Spirit of Truth to guide you into truth (John 14:16–17, 15:26, 16:7–15) as He transforms you. Your part in this transformation is summarized in 2 Corinthians 4:17–18 (NLT): "For our present troubles are small and won't last very long. Yet they produce for us a glory that vastly outweighs them and will last forever! So we don't look at the troubles we can see now; rather, we fix our gaze on things that cannot be seen. For the things we see now will soon be gone, but the things we cannot see will last forever."

In Matthew 6:25–34, Jesus teaches His disciples not to worry. In D. Martyn Lloyd-Jones' classic work *Studies in the Sermon on the Mount*, he notes that "Jesus' disciples were controlled by their circumstances rather than by the truth of Jesus' teaching." He goes on to tell us the following:

Faith, according to our Lord's teaching in this paragraph, is primarily thinking; and the whole trouble with a man of little faith is that he does not think. He allows circumstances to bludgeon him. That is the real difficulty in life. Life comes to us with a club in its hand and strikes us upon the head, and we become incapable of thought, helpless and defeated. The way to avoid that, according to our Lord, is to think. We must spend more time in studying our Lord's lessons in observation and deduction. The Bible is full of logic, and we must never think of faith as something purely mystical. We do not just sit down in an armchair and expect marvelous things to happen to us. That is not Christian faith. Christian faith is essentially thinking. Look at the birds, think about them, and draw your deductions. Look at the grass, look at the lilies of the field, consider them.

The trouble with most people, however, is that they will not think. Instead of doing this, they sit down and ask, What is going to happen to me? What can I do? That is the absence of thought; it is surrender, it is defeat. Our Lord, here, is urging us to think, and to think in a Christian manner. That is the very essence of faith. Faith, if you like, can be defined like this: It is a man insisting upon thinking when everything seems determined to bludgeon and knock him down in an intellectual sense. The trouble with the person of little faith is that, instead of controlling his own thought, his thought is being controlled by something else, and, as we put it, he goes round and round in circles. That is the essence of worry . . . That is not thought; that is the absence of thought, a failure to think.[vii]

One of the clearest examples in the Old Testament of someone living in truth rather than feeling was Father Abraham. Abraham was commanded by the Creator of the universe to sacrifice his only son, Isaac. This was the son Yahweh had promised to bless the entire world through, but how could that happen if he were dead? Abraham, Isaac, and two servants set out on their three-day journey from Beersheba to Mount Moriah, a distance of about fifty miles. Imagine the mental gymnastics Abraham went through all alone in his thoughts. Aside from Yahweh, neither Isaac nor the two servants knew about Abraham's divine assignment. Step by step, Abraham would have rehearsed Yahweh's promise regarding Isaac and Yahweh's command to sacrifice him. Imagine the images in Abraham's mind. His heart ached and trembled at the thought of thrusting a knife into his son's body; his feelings were intense! But on the other side was the truth of both Yahweh's promise and his command. Back and forth, feelings or truth—what would he decide?

For three long days, with every step, he pondered all this alone, without any human intervention, understanding, or counsel. How did he respond? How did he choose? Was his decision based on feelings or the truth of Yahweh's promises? We gain our first insight from Abraham's command to his two servants in Genesis 22:5: "And Abraham said to his young men, 'Stay here with the donkey while I and the boy go over there; and we will worship, and *we* will return to you'" (emphasis added). The second insight comes from Genesis 22:7–8, when Isaac asked Abraham where the sacrifice was: "'Behold, the fire and the wood, but where is the lamb for the burnt offering?' And Abraham said, 'God *will provide* for Himself the lamb for the burnt offering, my son'" (emphasis added). Abraham, in faith of God's promised words, not feelings, walks with his son, trusting he will return with Isaac to the two servants because Yahweh would provide. Living in Yahweh's truth, Abraham builds the altar, places his son on it, and raises his knife, still believing in truth and not his feelings. We know the rest of the story. Abraham was right to live in truth, not feelings, for Yahweh provided "a ram . . . caught in the thicket by its horns" (v. 13).

Praise God! Once again, He proves Himself faithful to those who live in truth!

One important truth I hope you accept is that your spiritual battle is part of God's plan to shape you into the character of Jesus. You are meant to fight for God's glory by avoiding all bondage and living in the freedom of His truth today. Nothing good comes from anxiety. You will face daily opportunities to worry—Monday worries, Tuesday worries, and so on. Instead, rely on God's mercies and lovingkindness, which are new every day (Lamentations 3:21–24; Psalm 94:19). Even if your life isn't going as you would like, make choices that promote His kingdom and righteousness, remembering that one day you will be with Him forever.

Anxiety reveals misplaced loyalties. Return to God's truth, which results in freedom. My friend Bill Sisterson wisely said, "The problem with anxiety is that you think you are doing something to fix the problem. If you take your eyes off Jesus, just like Peter, you won't walk on the water. Enjoy walking on the water and keep your focus on Jesus." Remember that your emotions are a choice. When feeling anxious, ask the Spirit to reveal the lie you're believing. Anxiety will pass, but the truth will remain (Matthew 24:35). You must avoid letting your worries become an idol. Another friend, Mike Kemp, said, "Take your anxiety captive. Don't allow your emotions to compete with God. This violates the first commandment." I wholeheartedly agree with their wisdom.

No matter what happens, Yahweh is your loving, heavenly Father, and He is in control. Do you trust Him? Do you truly know Him as your loving, heavenly Father? If so, talk to Him freely. Prayer helps you overcome anxiety (Philippians 4:6–7). There is nothing in life worth worrying about, and nothing is too small to pray about.

It's Only a Comma

Giving God your anxieties doesn't guarantee He will change your circumstances, but He will grant you peace when you hand them over to Him. God doesn't always provide an immediate solution, but He offers—as someone said "divine insulation from anxiety and fear." The issue isn't whether you have worries and fears—if you're honest, you do —but that's not the point. The question is, "What do you do with them?"

We are told what to do with our anxieties in 1 Peter 5:5–7,

> You younger men, likewise, be subject to your elders. And all of you, clothe yourselves with humility toward one another, for "God is opposed to the proud, but gives grace to the humble." [6]Therefore humble yourselves under the mighty hand of God, that He may exalt you at the proper time, [7]casting all your anxiety on Him, because He cares for you.

I memorized the above verses over fifty years ago. However, I recently realized that I had overlooked a very important punctuation mark—the comma between verse 6 and verse 7. In this section of Scripture, Peter teaches about humility, a crucial character trait in the Christian life. Peter goes on to say that we should cast our anxieties on God because God cares for us. But I missed that small comma. I thought Peter was starting a new idea about our anxiety, but I overlooked the vital link between humility and giving God my anxiety. In other words, Peter is saying that God wants you, in a spirit of humility, to give Him your worries and anxieties.

I never saw the connection, and once I discovered it, I often thought about it. One day, as I reflected on the comma, I wondered, "Why is it that after I pray and give God my anxiety, I often start worrying again in just minutes or even seconds?" I thought, "If God wants me to surrender my anxiety humbly, why do I keep taking it back?" This led me to an uncomfortable realization. In humility, I gave my anxiety to God, but then I took it back out of pride. I admitted, "Okay, God, I've given You my anxiety, but now I want it back. I guess, Lord, I don't fully trust You. I want to think about my problem, consider it, and keep working on how to handle it myself. Honestly, Lord, I don't like the idea of handing it over to You to do with as You will—I want to control it myself." What a foolish thing to think and do. Such pride! It honestly reminds me of Satan. I will write more about this in chapter six, titled "Freedom from Pride."

Some Names of God

Before I conclude this chapter, I want to share an activity that helps me when my trust in God is waning. I made a laminated card listing some of God's names, meanings, and Bible references. As I slowly read and pray over them, my trust in God is strengthened, and I am motivated to keep pressing on with Him in intimacy and humility. Here are fifteen examples from the New Living Translation:

1. **Elohim**: "In the beginning <u>God</u> created the heavens and the earth" (Genesis 1:1).

2. **El Elyon**: "Melchizedek blessed Abram with this blessing: 'Blessed be Abram by <u>God Most High</u>, Creator of heaven and earth'" (Genesis 14:19).

3. **Adon (or Adonay)**: "<u>O Sovereign Lord</u>, what good are all your blessings when I don't even have a son? Since you've given me no children, Eliezer of Damascus, a servant in my household, will inherit all my wealth" (Genesis 15:2).

4. **El Roi**: "Thereafter, Hagar used another name to refer to the Lord, who had spoken to her. She said, '<u>You are the God who sees me</u>.' She also said, 'Have I truly seen the One who sees me?'" (Genesis 16:13).

5. **El Shaddai**: "When Abram was ninety-nine years old, the LORD appeared to him and said, 'I am El-Shaddai—<u>God Almighty</u>.' Serve me faithfully and live a blameless life'" (Genesis 17:1).

6. **El Olam**: "Then Abraham planted a tamarisk tree at Beersheba, and there he worshiped the LORD, <u>the Eternal God</u>" (Genesis 21:33).

7. **Yahweh-Yireh**: "Then Abraham looked up and saw a ram caught by its horns in a thicket. So he took the ram and sacrificed it as a burnt offering in place of his son. Abraham named the place Yahweh-Yireh (which means '<u>the LORD will provide</u>'). To this day, people still use that name as a proverb: 'On the mountain of the LORD it will be provided'" (Genesis 22:13–14).

8. **Yahweh**: "But Moses protested, 'If I go to the people of Israel and tell them, "The God of your ancestors has sent me to you," they will ask me, "What is his name?" Then what should I tell them?' God replied to Moses, '<u>I AM WHO I AM</u>. Say this to the people of Israel: I AM has sent me to you'" (Exodus 3:13–14).

9. **Yahweh-Rapha**: "He said, 'If you will listen carefully to the voice of the LORD your God and do what is right in his sight, obeying his commands and keeping all his decrees, then I will not make you suffer any of the diseases I sent on the Egyptians; for I am <u>the LORD who heals you</u>'" (Exodus 15:26).

10. **Yahweh-Nissi**: "Moses built an altar there and named it Yahweh-nissi (which means '<u>the LORD is my banner</u>')" (Exodus 17:15).

11. **Yahweh-Mekoddishkem**: "Tell the people of Israel: 'Be careful to keep my Sabbath day, for the Sabbath is a sign of the covenant between me and you from generation to

generation. It is given so you may know that <u>I am the LORD, who makes you holy</u>.'" (Exodus 31:13).

12. **Yahweh-Shalom**: "And Gideon built an altar to the LORD there and named it Yahweh-Shalom (which means '<u>the LORD is peace</u>')" (Judges 6:24).

13. **Yahweh-Sabaoth**: "David replied to the Philistine, 'You come to me with sword, spear, and javelin, but I come to you in the name of <u>the LORD of Heaven's Armies</u>—the God of the armies of Israel, whom you have defied'" (1 Samuel 17:45).

14. **Yahweh-Raah**: "<u>The LORD is my shepherd</u>; I have all that I need" (Psalm 23:1).

15. **Yahweh-Tsidkenu**: "For the time is coming," says the LORD, "when I will raise up a righteous descendant from King David's line. He will be a King who rules with wisdom. He will do what is just and right throughout the land. And this will be his name: '<u>The LORD Is Our Righteousness</u>.' In that day Judah will be saved, and Israel will live in safety" (Jeremiah 23:5–6).

In conclusion, if you want to display the pride of the devil, keep your anxiety to yourself and all the ungodly fruit that comes with it. But if you want to be like your Savior in the Garden of Gethsemane, humbly surrender your anxiety to your heavenly Father, and trust that His will is best for you and His glory. Trust your Sovereign Father to handle it in His way and timing, even if it's not what you want. Remember, not my will but Yours be done (Luke 22:42). Submission to God destroys the power of anxiety. This is your choice.

I recommend listening to the encouraging song "Even If" by Mercy Me (2017).

Small-group Discussion Questions

1. Since Matthew 6:25–34 teaches that God has promised to supply all your needs, what benefit is there in worrying about tomorrow?

2. How does God's eternal sovereignty relate to your current anxiety?

3. You know what it feels like to focus on your worries; now, what is it like to focus on His rest amidst your worries?

Suggestions for Freedom from Worry

1. Your life reflects what you think about (Proverbs 23:7). So, choose to stop dwelling on your worries and instead focus on what is true, honorable, right, pure, lovely, and admirable (Philippians 4:8).

2. Instead of giving in to worry, choose to worship and praise your Father, the King of the universe, and remember He has promised to use this for your good (Romans 8:28).

3. You already have the ability to walk in truth by:
    a. Clearly expressing your worries.
    b. Humbly casting your worries on God.
    c. Not taking back what you have just given to God.

Chapter Six

FREEDOM FROM PRIDE

Therefore humble yourselves under the mighty hand of God, that He may exalt you at the proper time.
1 PETER 5:6

As we move on to another topic, remember that pride and humility are choices based on your deepest desires. As I mentioned in chapter three on renewing your mind, we may be unaware of our deepest desires. Still, you need to take the time to identify the desire that naturally leads to pride in your thoughts, speech, and interactions with others. This is an important step in growing in personal holiness, supported by prayer and reliance on the Holy Spirit.

Let's begin our study on overcoming pride by examining two perfect examples that can shed light on our response to Peter's command in 1 Peter 5:6. First, we will look at Lucifer's perfect example of pride, followed by Yahweh's response to the devil's choice. Then, we will consider Jesus' perfect humility and how His heavenly Father responded to Jesus' decision.

Prideful Creatures

The just God of the universe will punish all sin throughout His entire creation. His anger and righteousness will target Satan, his demons, and all sinful humanity. At times in the Old Testament, the prophets combined God's work among local people with His actions in the spiritual realm. This connection is clear in Isaiah 13:1–14:23 and 21:1–10, especially concerning the ancient city of Babylon. The ruins of Babylon are located in present-day Iraq.

We find in Isaiah (13:6, 9, 13) that the prophet not only foresees the fall of Babylon but also glimpses a shadow of the day of the Lord, when God unleashes His wrath on the earth (v. 11). This prophecy is also shown in Revelation 17–18, where the evil world system of Babylon is destroyed. It's important to understand that Babylon not only refers to the ancient city in Iraq but also symbolizes the evil systems of the world in contrast to the holy city of Jerusalem (Isaiah 13:19; Revelation 18:2–8). According to John Oswalt:

> Some of the church fathers, linking this passage (Isaiah 14:12–15) to Luke 10:18 and Revelation 12:8, 9, took it to refer to the fall of Satan described in those places. However, the great expositors of the Reformation were unanimous in arguing that the context here does not support such an interpretation. This passage is discussing human pride, which, while monumental to be sure, is still human and not angelic . . . The remarkable thing about the Isaiah passage is that the challenge is by a human being . . . Ultimately, the battle is between Creator and creatures, and the issue is whether we will accord him the right due him as Creator and bow to him in glad service or will continue to insist that we are as he is and continue to have our arrogance mocked by the worm.[i]

Even though some commentators believe this passage only refers to humanity, if so, that prideful humanity would still be influenced by this delusional notion given by the devil: "I will be like the Most High" (Isaiah 14:14).

Warren W. Wiersbe makes the following observations:

> The picture in Isaiah 14:1–23 is that of a mighty monarch whose pride brought him to destruction. This is what happened to Belshazzar when

Darius the Mede captured Babylon in 539 B.C. (Daniel 5). Isaiah described the king's arrival in Sheol, the world of the dead, where the king's wealth, glory, and power vanished. The dead kings already in Sheol stood in tribute to him (Isaiah 14:9), but it was all a mockery. Death is the great leveler; there are no kings in the world of the dead. "Lucifer" (v. 12) is Latin for "morning star" and suggests that this king's glory did not last very long. The morning star shines but is soon swallowed up by the light of the sun.[ii]

I believe Isaiah sees more in this passage than just the defeat of the king of Babylon; he also predicts the defeat and eternal judgment of Satan (prince of this world) and his demons, who empower and deceive the leaders of the world to oppose God and His people (John 12:31; Ephesians 2:1–3).

Here, we see highlighted the perfect pride of Satan in Isaiah's description of the devil's arrogant focus on himself, which is also common among sinful humanity. We observe in Isaiah 14:13–14 Satan's attempt to elevate himself to the same level as the King of Glory while demanding the world's praise and worship (Matthew 4:8–10; Revelation 13:4, 8, 12). Satan tries to attain this unworthy worship by imitating Jesus Christ (Isaiah 14:14; 2 Corinthians 11:13–15). The devil does this through his puppet, the Antichrist. However, just as the king of Babylon was humiliated and defeated, so, too, Satan will be crushed by King Jesus and cast into the eternal lake of fire (Revelation 20:10).

Here are the king's (and Satan's) five prideful statements recorded in Isaiah 14:13–14; notice his preoccupation with himself, shown by his repeated use of "I."

1. "But you said in your heart, 'I will ascend to heaven; (v. 13)

2. I will raise my throne above the stars of God, (v. 13)

3. And I will sit on the mount of assembly in the recesses of the north. (v. 13)

4. I will ascend above the heights of the clouds; (v. 14)

5. I will make myself like the Most High.'" (v. 14)

Not only do we see Lucifer's pride, but we also notice in verse 13 his self-centeredness—"But you said in your heart." His pride was his greatest inclination, reflected in how he chose to live.

Whether Isaiah's passage refers only to humanity or also includes Satan, the battle remains between the Creator of the universe and His creatures—angels and humans. There is no hope for Satan and his demons, but are you living a God-centered or self-centered life? Your words and actions always stem from your greatest inclinations. Remember, the just God deals with Satan, demons, and sinful humans alike, as recorded in Proverbs 16:18: "Pride goes before destruction, and a haughty spirit before stumbling."

Yahweh's Response

We now review Yahweh's, the Creator's, punishment of Lucifer and the king of Babylon in Isaiah 14:12–19. After examining each verse, I will share a brief comment.

1. "How you have fallen from heaven, O star of the morning, son of the dawn! You have been cut down to the earth, you who have weakened the nations" (v. 12)! The one who controlled the world's powers and rendered them weak will soon face even greater weakness.

2. "Nevertheless you will be brought down to Sheol, to the recesses of the pit" (v. 15). Yahweh has sentenced this prideful individual to the realm of the dead. Anyone seeking godhood or God's throne will face eternal emptiness and insignificance.

3. "Those who see you will gaze at you, they will carefully consider you, saying, 'Is this the man who made the earth tremble, who caused kingdoms to quake'" (v. 16)? Those in Sheol mock this one, for there is no king or leader in the place of judgment. This mighty one has been cast into a terrible, eternal, and disgraceful place. This once-glorious, powerful king arrives in the land of the dead, stripped of all his former proud possessions and authority.

4. "Who made the world like a wilderness and pulled down its cities, who did not allow his prisoners to go home" (v. 17)? The one who would not permit his enemies to return to their homes is now eternally homeless.

5. "All the kings of the nations lie in glory, each in his own place" (v. 18). Luke 4:5–7 shows that all the kingdoms of the world, including Babylon, belong to Satan. In the future, Babylon will represent the evil systems of the entire world. Unlike many earthly kings who have received honorable burials, the king of Babylon and the devil will not.

6. "But you have been cast out of your grave like an abhorred branch, clothed with those killed who are pierced with a sword, who go down to the stones of the pit like a trampled corpse" (v. 19). This king is reduced to a most dishonorable state, a corpse crushed beneath the living's feet.

God's Humble Servant

After reading a description of our Savior's choice of humility, we will explore the perfect humility of our incarnate Redeemer.

> Doing nothing from selfish ambition or vain glory, but with humility of mind regarding one another as more important than yourselves, not merely looking out for your own personal interests, but also for the interests of others. Have this way of thinking in yourselves which was also in Christ Jesus, who, although existing in the form of God, did not regard equality with God a thing to be grasped, but emptied Himself, by taking the form of a slave, by being made in the likeness of men. Being found in appearance as a man, He humbled Himself by becoming obedient to the point of death, even death on a cross.
> Philippians 2:3–8

The passage above clearly illustrates Jesus' humility in fulfilling the work of our redemption. Verse 3 shows that Jesus' humility began in his mind. Genuine outward humility must first be an internal reality. Verse 5 continues the same idea: humility is a way of thinking—a way of understanding ourselves in relation to God and others.

1. As the God-Man, "with humility of mind." In other words, true outward humility was initially a reality in His mind.

2. "[He] did not regard equality with God a thing to be grasped." Jesus' divine nature is unchangeable and cannot be altered or taken away. Before coming to earth, He coexisted as Yahweh and was equal with God the Father and God the Spirit in every way (John 10:30). He was, is, and always will be the unchanging God. Yet, He didn't cling to these truths but chose to set them aside to serve humanity by redeeming the elect.

3. "[Jesus] emptied Himself." Jesus, the Creator and owner of all, chose to set aside the following:
   a. Any form of control or use of His creation for His benefit, except His deity.
   b. The visible display of His glory, which becomes clear when His human brothers did not recognize who He was (John 7:5).
   c. The independent expression of His will, only doing the will of His Father (John 5:30, 6:38, Matthew 26:39–44).
   d. The independent sharing of His insights and performing miracles; instead, He relied solely on what the Father and Spirit provided Him (John 1:47–48, 2:25, 5:19–23, 26; Matthew 24:36, 39–44).
   e. All His prerogatives and riches in heaven (2 Corinthians 8:9).
   f. His intimate, face-to-face relationship with His Father, which, to pay for His people's sins, led Him to become sin on our behalf (2 Corinthians 5:21).
   g. His moment-by-moment communion with His Father on the cross (Matthew 27:46).
   h. Aspects of His omniscience. "But of that day and hour no one knows, not even the angels of heaven, nor the

Son, but the Father alone" (Matthew 24:36; Mark 13:32).

"[Jesus took] the form of a slave." Why would the King of the universe take the form of a slave? It's beyond our understanding; yet, it remains true. He chose to submit to His Father and the Holy Spirit by doing what they directed because He loves you (John 3:16) and wants you with Him forever (Psalm 73:26; John 14:3, 17:24). In the following, John MacArthur explains the implications of Jesus' choice to become a slave:

A doulos (bond-servant) owned nothing, not even the clothes on his back. Everything he had, including his life, belonged to his master. Jesus owned His own clothes, but He owned no land or house, no gold or jewels. He owned no business, no boat, and no horse. He had to borrow a donkey when He rode into Jerusalem on Palm Sunday, borrow a room for the Last Supper, and even was buried in a borrowed tomb. He refused any property, any advantages, any special service to Himself. Relative to His glory, the King of Kings and Lord of Lords willingly became the Bond-servant of bond-servants. The one who "was in the beginning with God" and through whom "all things came into being" (John 1:2–3) claimed as His own nothing that He had created. Among other things, a bond-servant was required to carry other people's burdens. As the supreme Bond-servant, Jesus carried the burden that no other man could carry, the sin-burden for all who would believe. As Isaiah revealed, "The Lord has caused the iniquity of us all to fall on Him" (Isaiah 53:6).[iii]

4. "Being found in appearance as a man." Even though Jesus was like pre-fall Adam, having no sin. He possessed a genuine human body that included all the limitations, weaknesses, problems, and abilities to suffer brought on by Adam's sin (Romans 8:3). Additionally, Jesus had the ability to sin (like pre-fall Adam) and was tempted in all things as we are (Hebrews 4:15; Matthew 4:1–11), yet He chose not to sin. The fact that Jesus lived for thirty-three years as the God-Man, with the ability to sin, yet chose not to sin, supports the truth of Hebrews 2:18: "For since He Himself was tempted in that which He has suffered, He can come to

help those who are tempted." Therefore, this made Him "the Lamb of God, who takes away the sin of the world" (John 1:29). Finally, because He was fully and truly man and fully and truly God, He could die for the sins of those who trust in Him, thereby satisfying God's wrath against His followers (propitiation, Hebrews 2:17). Praise God!

5. "[Jesus] humbled Himself by becoming obedient to the point of death, even death on a cross." Not only did the Son of God humble Himself as God, but He also humbled Himself further as a man. It was necessary for Jesus to assume human nature and become the God-Man, but additional humility was required for the salvation of the saints. In humility, He chose to allow His creatures, both Jews and Gentiles, to falsely accuse, arrest, and mistreat Him. This led to His being mocked, beaten with fists, scourged with a whip, spat upon, and having parts of His beard pulled out. Not only did this man, who was God, permit these unjust actions, but in humility, He never responded with threats, accusations, or promises of retribution (1 Peter 2:23). The greatest and final display of Jesus' humility was His submission to death. This act brought eternal salvation to every Christian, for we are told in Romans 5:19, "For as through the one man's disobedience the many were appointed sinners, even so through the obedience of the One the many will be appointed righteous." Jesus' humility leads to our glorification with Him forever (Romans 8:17; Colossians 3:4). It's amazing that Adam's choice, made in a moment based on a lie, brought a curse upon all humanity, while Jesus' choice, made before the foundation of the world, based on the truth, was unimaginably costly. Adam's choice served himself, whereas Jesus' choice served His Father, resulting in eternal blessing for Christians. The implications of our choices can be profound, so be deliberate in living in the freedom of the truth.

God the Father's Response to the Humility of His Son

How does Jesus' holy Father respond to His Son's perfect humility, as demonstrated throughout His redemptive work? The following passages describe the many blessings the Father has given His Son because of His humble and perfect work:

1. "Therefore, God also highly exalted Him, and bestowed on Him the name which is above every name, so that at the name of Jesus every knee will bow, of those who are in heaven and on earth and under the earth, and that every tongue will confess that Jesus Christ is LORD, to the glory of God the Father" (Philippians 2:9–11).

2. "[Jesus] who, having accomplished cleansing for sins, sat down at the right hand of the Majesty on high, having become so much better than the angels, as He has inherited a more excellent name than they" (Hebrews 1:3b–4).

3. "Which He worked in Christ, by raising Him from the dead and seating Him at His right hand in the heavenly places, far above all rule and authority and power and dominion, and every name that is named, not only in this age but also in the one to come. And He put all things in subjection under His feet, and gave Him as head over all things to the church, which is His body, the fullness of Him who fills all in all" (Ephesians 1:20–23).

4. "And to Him was given dominion, glory, and a kingdom, that all the peoples, nations, and men of every tongue might serve Him. His dominion is an everlasting dominion, which will not be taken away; and His kingdom is one which will not be destroyed" (Daniel 7:14).

5. "Therefore having been exalted to the right hand of God, and having received from the Father the promise of the Holy Spirit, He has poured out this which you both see and hear. For David did not ascend into the heavens, but he himself says: 'The LORD said to my Lord, 'Sit at My right hand,

until I put Your enemies as a footstool for Your feet.'
Therefore let all the house of Israel know for certain that
God has made Him both Lord and Christ—this Jesus
whom you crucified" (Acts 2:33–36).

6. "[Jesus] who is at the right hand of God, having gone into
   heaven, after angels and authorities and powers had been
   subjected to Him" (1 Peter 3:22).

7. "And from Jesus Christ, the faithful witness, the firstborn of
   the dead, and the ruler of the kings of the earth. To Him
   who loves us and released us from our sins by His blood—
   and He has made us to be a kingdom, priests to His God
   and Father—to Him be the glory and the might forever and
   ever. Amen. Behold, He is coming with the clouds, and
   every eye will see Him, even those who pierced Him; and all
   the tribes of the earth will mourn over Him. Yes, amen. 'I
   am the Alpha and the Omega,' says the Lord God, 'who is
   and who was and who is to come, the Almighty.'" . . . "And
   in the middle of the lampstands I saw one like a son of man,
   clothed in a robe reaching to the feet, and girded across His
   chest with a golden sash. And His head and His hair were
   white like white wool, like snow; and His eyes were like a
   flame of fire" (Revelation 1:5–8, 13–14).

8. Jesus is called faithful and true, and in righteousness, He
   judges and wages war. His eyes are like flames of fire, and on
   His head are many diadems; He has a name written on Him
   that no one knows except Himself. Jesus comes to earth
   riding a white horse, accompanied by the armies in heaven,
   which include angels (Matthew 25:31) and saints (1
   Thessalonians 3:13; Jude 14–15; Revelation 17:14, 19:11–
   14), with a sharp sword and iron rod. He has the name King
   of Kings and Lord of Lords written on him. This is all
   followed by Jesus' throwing the Antichrist and the False
   Prophet into the lake of fire forever (Revelation 19:15–16,
   19–20).

9. Jesus reigns on earth for one thousand years (Revelation 20:1–6).

10. Jesus defeats and condemns Satan to the eternal lake of fire (Revelation 20:7–10).

11. Jesus, at His Great White Throne Judgment, will sentence all the lost, death, and Hades to the lake of fire for eternity (Revelation 20:11–15).

12. Jesus, together with His Father and the Holy Spirit, reigns forever in the new heaven and earth (Revelation 21–22).

The above illustrates humility triumphing over pride. Both Jesus and Satan chose their paths, and we have seen God's response to their decisions. Now, let's spend the rest of this chapter reflecting on how you will choose.

The Father's Expectations for His Son's Disciples

We first examined Satan's pride in its perfection, and then the perfection of Jesus' humility. The question is, "Whose example will you choose to follow?" The answer is found in the same passage that describes our Lord's choice of humility, Philippians 2:3–4: "Do nothing from selfish ambition or vain glory, but with humility of mind regarding one another as more important than yourselves, not merely looking out for your own personal interests, but also for the interests of others."

Here in Philippians 2:3–4, Yahweh commands you to think and live like Jesus, just as we learned in Philippians 2:5: "Have this way of thinking in yourselves which was also in Christ Jesus." Your heavenly Father intends for you to live like Jesus, your Lord and Savior. His command relates to your thinking. This command is not only about what you think, but also how you think. In other words, it concerns both the content of your thoughts and the process of thinking. Therefore, in the following numbered list, let's explore how we can incorporate Jesus' humble lifestyle into our everyday lives.

1. Jesus' humility started in His mind. In other words, His
   outward humility first existed in His thoughts. God wants
   you to develop genuine humility as a natural part of your
   life. God's main command is to choose to humble yourself
   through self-denial (Luke 9:23). This becomes evident when
   you focus more on the needs of others than your own
   (Matthew 22:39). True humility cannot be visible in your
   life unless it first resides in your mind. It happens when you
   submit to God and surrender your will to His (James 4:7).

   But it's important to recognize that God's will is directly
   tied to the truth of His Word. Denying yourself is a choice
   that must stem from your focus on truth, not your feelings,
   even when your feelings are positive. Many people make
   choices based on positive feelings; however, when your
   greatest inclination is a lie, those positive feelings are also
   based on a lie. To deny yourself means your starting point is
   not you and your feelings, but Jesus, who is the Truth (John
   14:6) and your Lord (2 Peter 1:14). There is no other way to
   deny yourself. Denying yourself is not a focus on a pathway
   of good feelings, just as living in the truth is not following a
   path but rather the person of Jesus Christ.

2. He did not see equality with God as something to cling to.
   The selfless attitude Jesus demonstrated is precisely what
   God wants you to adopt. Just as Jesus obeyed the Father's
   will and did everything He was instructed to do, you are also
   to follow whatever Jesus tells you in His Word. Therefore, as
   His slave (the true meaning of *servant/doulos*, in Philippians
   2:7), every day you are to deny yourself, take up your cross (a
   symbol of death), and follow Jesus wherever He leads (Luke
   9:23). Practically, this attitude is shown by how you choose
   to use your time, talents, gifts, money, and possessions—the
   things God has entrusted to you—to serve others for Jesus'
   sake (2 Corinthians 4:5). Remember, He owns all your
   temporary blessings, and you should imitate Jesus'
   willingness to sacrifice any or all of them for His glory and
   the benefit of others.

3. He emptied himself. Two truths to remember: First, you entered this world with nothing material and will leave the same way. Second, you were created by Him and for Him (Colossians 1:16). Therefore, every ability and possession Jesus has loaned to you is meant to be used as He directs and for His glory. I admit that when I lend a tool to someone, and it is returned broken or dirty, I wonder why anyone would show such disrespect. But isn't this precisely what we do when we choose to use what the Lord has loaned to us in a way that displeases Him? Additionally, this is also true when we receive praise and take credit for ourselves without giving credit to our Lord. When you are not self-centered but God-centered, you can freely direct praise given to you to the true source of what is being acknowledged about you. You can, in humility, confess the truth of Luke 17:10: "In this way, you also, when you do all the things which are commanded of you, say, 'We are unworthy slaves; we have done only that which we ought to have done.'" Therefore, when praise comes to you, see yourself as a conduit to pass on that praise to the only One who is praiseworthy (John 13:14–17). As someone once said, "We live for an audience of One." This is precisely how Jesus lived—for the audience of His Father (John 5:30, 6:38; Matthew 26:39–44). We are called to imitate Jesus' life and live solely for His audience and approval. He always sees why, what, and how we do something, and that should be enough to keep us loving and serving Him. Whose praise do we seek—men's or God's (John 12:43)?

   Another benefit of being God-centered is contentment. Paul told young Timothy, "But godliness actually is a means of great gain, when accompanied by contentment" (1 Timothy 6:6). Who would have guessed that emptying yourself for the sake of God's glory could lead to godliness and contentment? How opposite this is to the lies the world and the devil tell us. This is just another example of the freedom available to us when we choose to live in the truth.

4. He took the form of a slave by being made in the likeness of men. Jesus would never have descended to earth if He had

been thinking only about Himself. This is why He wants you to treat others as more important than yourself, just like Jesus treated you as more important than Himself. He demonstrated the worth and value of his disciples the night before He was crucified by modeling humility (Luke 22:27), by washing their feet, and by teaching them the need for ongoing forgiveness (John 13:4–5, 12–17). This is the attitude Jesus wanted to see in his disciples and in our lives today. Think about the humility of Jesus as you read Paul Rees' observations:

Look at Him—this amazing Jesus! He is helping Joseph make a yoke in that little carpenter's shop at Nazareth. This is the One who, apart from His self-emptying, could far more easily make a solar system or a galaxy of systems. Look at Him again! Dressed like a slave, with towel and basin for His menial equipment, He is bathing the feet of some friends of His who, but for their quarrelsomeness, should have been washing His feet . . . "He humbled himself!" "Don't forget this," cries Paul to these dear friends of his at Philippi. "Don't forget this when the slightest impulse arises to become self-assertive and self-seeking, and so to break the bond of your fellowship with one another!"[iv]

5. As a man, He humbled Himself by obeying His heavenly Father, including dying on a cross. You have been crucified with Jesus; positionally, you are dead to self and called to live that way practically (Galatians 2:20). Jesus died to self, yet He is the God Most High (El Elyon, Genesis 14:19). For your sake, Jesus became sin (2 Corinthians 5:21). He became the lowest of all humans to bring you to heaven so you can share in His eternal glory (Romans 8:17; 2 Thessalonians 2:14; Colossians 3:4). Remember, you were created by God and for God; therefore, don't turn away from Him in pride like the devil. Every time you think of yourself pridefully or act out of pride, you are acting like Lucifer. Pride is a form of bondage—bondage to sin and self-centeredness, which we have seen in Satan. According to Matthew 23:11–12, humility is a choice, but remember it must be your greatest inclination, rooted in prayer and God's Word. You are commanded to humble yourself, but if

you choose not to, your loving, heavenly Father will humble you (Matthew 23:12), for humility is essential to becoming like Jesus (1 Peter 1:15–16). Instead of following your enemy, the prideful Prince of Darkness, follow the humble Light of the World, for He has told you, "I am the Light of the world; he who follows Me will never walk in the darkness, but will have the Light of life" (John 8:12). As you humbly walk in the light, you will not rely on feelings but on truth and will therefore enjoy the Light of life (Psalm 16:11). Since you are a child of light (Ephesians 5:8), don't forget that your Master has promised to lift you up and to make you a participant in His eternal and glorious kingdom.

Does Water Freeze at 35°?

Imagine checking your phone for the weather, and it shows today's low will be 35°, but it will feel like 30°. Since it will feel like 30°, do you believe the water will freeze? Why or why not? Did you answer the question based on your feelings (30°) or the fact (35°)? Which is the wiser choice for determining whether water will freeze: following the facts or following your feelings? We readily recognize that we should live in truth, but when we are accused of things we have not done, are misrepresented, or face persecution for doing right, humility is not always our foremost inclination. But remember, your ability to choose humility still remains—just like it did with Jesus in the garden and on the cross. His greatest desire was to obey His Father, so He chose to do so. Consider asking yourself throughout the day, "Am I self-centered or God-centered?"

In chapter three, we discussed the concept of choice and its relationship to our greatest inclination. For Christians, by God's grace, we can choose either the table of sin or the table of righteousness. The idea of choice is widely understood, but we often overlook the long-term implications of the choices we are about to make. Let's consider for a moment the instructions Moses gave to the Israelites as they were about to enter the promised land, recorded in Deuteronomy 11:26–28:

See, I am setting before you today a blessing and a curse: the blessing, if
you listen to the commandments of Yahweh your God, which I am
commanding you today; and the curse, if you do not listen to the
commandments of Yahweh your God, but turn aside from the way
which I am commanding you today, by walking after other gods which
you have not known.

Moses instructs Israel at a pivotal moment in their national history.
They were about to enter the promised land, and Moses emphasized the
foundational truth of obedience to Yahweh. Moses presents two
options: blessings or a curse. The fruits of blessings would include life,
population growth, prosperity, abundance, and security in the land
(Deuteronomy 30:15–20). These were the promised fruits of choosing
to obey their God. However, if they chose to disobey, Yahweh would
bring a curse upon them. The fruit of this curse would include
Yahweh's displeasure, as evidenced by discipline and the loss of all the
aforementioned blessings, including their land. This would result in
people who looked no different than the Gentiles they were told to
remove from the land (Deuteronomy 28:15–68).

Considering Deuteronomy 30:19–20, in verse 19, Moses character-
izes the blessings and the curse as life and death. That's quite a choice!

I call heaven and earth to witness against you today, that I have set
before you life and death, the blessing and the curse. So choose life in
order that you may live, you and your seed...

In verse 20, we find what Yahweh really wants from His people:

By loving Yahweh your God, by listening to His voice, and by holding
fast to Him; for this is your life and the length of your days, that you
may live in the land which Yahweh swore to your fathers, to Abraham,
to Isaac, and to Jacob, to give them.

Do you see that life is what Yahweh wants for you and that it can be
experienced only through a loving relationship with Him? This requires
keeping your eyes on Him and listening to Him (living in the freedom
of the truth). Israel did not choose obedience and remains in bondage to
this day. But as followers of Jesus, we have the freedom to choose obedience every day of our lives. We may choose our way, the way of pride
and God's discipline, or Yahweh's way, the way of humility and blessing.

Just don't forget that Israel chose the road of pride, their way, and they lost everything. They were not willing to deny themselves. Pride is the sin of self-worship, as we have seen in Lucifer. Whom do you choose to imitate—Lucifer, the perfection of pride, or Jesus, the perfection of humility?

This passage from Deuteronomy highlights the importance of making the right choice "today" by choosing truth over emotion. It calls for following the One True Yahweh rather than the idol of self. As we have seen, Yahweh wants a loving relationship, but it comes with boundaries that your Creator knows are best for you. Remember, freedom is not the ability to do whatever you want, but being enabled to be who God wants you to be and to do what He wants you to do. God's boundaries are given to protect, guide, and bless you with peace and joy. When you accept your feelings as truth, you are worshiping yourself and turning away from the God of truth. What matters more to you, the praise of man or the praise of God (John 12:43)?

Choosing to Love People

In 2 John 2-4, John encourages believers to walk in truth in their relationships with one another. They are to love each other, as shown in John 13:34–35. The word *love* that John uses is the Greek term *agapáō*. Take the time to read 1 Corinthians 13:4–7 and see how this type of love is not based on feelings but on truth. This is the same kind of love Jesus has for each Christian (John 13:34–35). What kept Jesus on the cross? Was it truth or feelings? We see from 1 Corinthians 13:4–7 that agapáō is a choice based on truth rather than feelings. As Jesus was hanging on the cross, what do you think were some of His feelings? The answer is recorded in Isaiah 53. He was despised, forsaken, full of grief, and people hid their faces from Him (v. 3). And let's not forget the excruciating pain from the nails in His hands and feet. But He was also smitten, afflicted, chastened, and crushed by His loving, heavenly Father (vv. 4–5). In light of Jesus' punishment by man and God, along with the physical and emotional pain, because of His love for you, He chose to stay on the cross; yet, at any moment, He could have called down twelve legions of angels to remove Him (Matthew 26:53). But He remembered the truth of why He came to earth (John

12:27). He came to suffer on our behalf so we might be with Him forever.

So, why are you here on earth? "So that you may proclaim the excellencies of Him who has called you out of darkness into His marvelous light" (1 Peter 2:9). To do this, you need to deny yourself, take up your cross, and follow Jesus (Luke 9:23). This is what it means that you have been made by Him and for Him: You were created to glorify Him, which can only be accomplished when you live in the truth. Even though you are told that you will face trials, suffering, and persecution (2 Timothy 3:12; 1 Peter 4:12–13), you will not endure these by focusing on feelings, but as Jesus, you choose to live in the truth and accept the cup your Father has given you (John 18:11).

Pride and Anxiety: A Sinful Pairing

At the end of chapter five, "Freedom from Worry," we examined the connection between anxiety and pride. I sincerely handed my worry over to the Creator of the universe, and within seconds, I was worried again! Sometimes, we have feelings of pride and anxiety together. They're not identical, but often pride closely follows anxiety.

As we discussed that crucial comma in 1 Peter 5:5–7, humility is essential to giving your worries to God. You can't give your worries to God in pride, but you can try to take them back from Him in pride. We are told in Proverbs 28:25, "An arrogant man stirs up strife; but he who trusts in Yahweh will be blessed." If you believe Jesus' grace is enough (2 Corinthians 12:9), you won't need pride. The person who trusts in Yahweh remains humble and cannot be prideful. The one who walks in humility recognizes that he has issues and limitations and needs God's help. Admitting your problem with pride and your inability to fix it is an expression of a broken and contrite heart—the heart of a humble person. Prideful people often refuse to admit they have issues or needs, and if they do, they rarely seek anyone's help, especially God's. Daring to deny oneself is essential for humility (Galatians 2:20).

Christians have no reason to be proud. You can live a humble and secure life because you have received God's promised provisions. "Faith is the assurance of things hoped for, the conviction of things not seen" (Hebrews 11:1). In other words, walking by faith means making humble decisions based on God's truth. This is how you live in God's reality instead of in the darkness of pride. God is trustworthy for your past, present, and future, because He is the only One who sees everything from a 360° perspective.

God loves humility in His children, but He opposes pride in everyone. Therefore, Peter commands you to humble yourself (1 Peter 5:5) so that God may lift you up. Once again, we see Augustine's prayer to God to enable him to do what He commands. Are you asking the Lord to free you from pride, or are you merely thinking about it? If you're thinking, consider this truth: in your act of pride, protecting your self-interest and reputation are most important. When you're prideful, you are unlike your humble Savior, but you are exactly like Lucifer. Don't be deceived; pride might be closer to your anxiety than you realize.

Doubt Yourself?

Doubting yourself might not seem wise, and the world doesn't offer this advice. However, the Bible presents a very different view of how to see yourself when making decisions. Does that surprise you? Consider Proverbs 3:5–6, which says, "Trust in Yahweh with all your heart and do not lean on your own understanding. In all your ways acknowledge Him, and He will make your paths straight." I discussed these verses in chapter three on renewing your mind, but here I want to briefly highlight a point by G. K. Chesterton that, when practiced, can be very freeing. "A man was meant to be doubtful about himself, but undoubting about the truth; this has been reversed. Nowadays, the part of a man that a man does assert is exactly the part he ought not to assert—himself. The part he doubts is exactly the part he ought not to doubt."[v]

It's important to remember that God's intention for humanity is a constant dependence on Him, not independence. Many Christians quickly acknowledge their dependence on God when facing a problem, but once God resolves the issue, these same Christians often live as if they are independent. Hosea highlights this very issue: "But when you had eaten and were satisfied, you became proud and forgot me" (Hosea 13:6 NLT).

Fundamentally, pride and humility are directly linked to where one finds satisfaction and contentment. Paul told Timothy that "godliness actually is a means of great gain, when accompanied by contentment" (1 Timothy 6:6). You will experience freedom if your daily pursuit is godliness and contentment with your present state and circumstances.

The common denominator of pride is self-worship. If your satisfaction and contentment come from yourself, then you are filled with self and pride. But if your satisfaction and contentment are in Jesus, you are filled with the Spirit, and, therefore, are living in a humble, abiding relationship with Jesus (John 15:5; Galatians 5:22–23). To live in Christ is to acknowledge that God is sovereign over every one of your circumstances. When you believe He loves you and is good, this acknowledgment will lead to freedom. He has always been in control, and it is wise to accept and live in this freedom every day of your life.

John Piper offers these insights:

> As long as we have the itch of self-regard, we shall want the pleasure of self-approval; but the happiest moments are those when we forget our precious selves and have neither but have everything else (God), instead. The itch of self-regard craves the scratch of self-approval. That is, if we are getting our pleasure from feeling self-sufficient, we will not be satisfied without others seeing and applauding our self-sufficiency.[vi] Itching for glory from other people makes faith impossible. Why? Because faith is being satisfied with all that God is for you in Jesus; and if you are bent on getting the satisfaction of your itch from the scratch of others' acclaim, you will turn away from Jesus.[vii]

I suggest listening to "Clothe Me in Humility" by Ken Bible (2000).

Small-group Discussion Questions

1. How can you shift from being self-centered to God-centered?

2. What is at the heart of your life that longs for self-approval?

3. How do you "not lean on your own understanding" (Proverbs 3:5)?

Suggestions for Freedom from Pride

1. Throughout your day, ask yourself, "Am I God-centered or self-centered?"

2. When feeling prideful, ask yourself why you want to imitate Lucifer rather than Jesus.

3. What do you need to let go of to grow in humility?

Chapter Seven

FREEDOM FROM FEAR

*Do not fear, for I am with you; do not anxiously look about you, for I am
your God. I will make you mighty, surely I will help you; surely I will
uphold you with My righteous right hand.*
ISAIAH 41:10

The High Dive of Fear

As a college student arriving on Penn State's main campus, I was
exploring the large grounds when I saw the big swimming pool. The
pool had three different heights for platform diving, and I felt the challenge ahead—especially at the highest level. So, I suited up and went to
the five-meter platform. The lifeguard, who was giving permission to
divers on all three platforms, looked at me and asked, "Is one ready?" I
replied, "One is ready," and then dove into the pool. I still had two more
levels to conquer. I climbed to the 7.5-meter platform, and when it was
my turn, the lifeguard asked, "Is two ready?" I said, "Two is ready," and
dove into the sparkling water. Next, I started climbing the steps of the
ten-meter platform. As I think about this scary event, it reminds me of
Jacob's ladder reaching heaven. When I finally reached the top, I was
amazed—I could see all over campus! I carefully walked to the edge and
looked down at the water. For some reason, the pool looked much
smaller. Then I heard the lifeguard call out, "Is three ready?" I looked

down slowly and was reminded of how important honesty is, so I said, "Three is not ready!" He was patient with me, maybe too patient. The view from up there was stunning until I looked back down at the tiny pool. I slowly approached the very edge, using binoculars to look down at the lifeguard. When I zoomed in, I saw him smiling as he asked, "Is three ready?" Standing there, scared by what might happen, I said, "Three is ready!" I placed my toes over the edge, leaned forward until I couldn't stop falling, and then pushed off as gravity took over. I executed a perfect duck dive while eating some grapes on the way down. I sliced through the water like a brick and then, slowly but surely, made my way to the side. It was over—the dive and my fear.

A report on mental toughness noted the following,

A recent study published on August 5, 2025, investigated the psychological states of elite athletes and found that the fear experienced during high-pressure competition shares significant similarities with the fear of death . . . The research indicates that the fear and anxiety experienced by elite athletes in competitive environments are not merely performance-related stress but can be psychologically intense, akin to the fear of death, due to the significant personal and professional stakes involved.[i]

There are two connected factors from my diving experience and sports psychology research. First, according to the research, even if an athlete does not believe his sporting event will lead to his physical death, the fear he feels can be the same type of fear as if he thought he were going to die. Second, this highlights the importance of athletes undergoing mental toughness training to reduce or eliminate their fear and anxiety about an upcoming or anticipated event. What does this have to do with the fear you experience throughout your life, even if it's not related to sports? We will see that David's mental toughness is a clear example of living in the truth, rather than being driven by fearful feelings. This was not something David was born with, but rather something he learned through knowing and obeying the truth of God's Word. This choice enabled David to run toward Goliath while the lie of fear caused Israel's army to stand frozen in place.

In 1 Samuel 17, we learn about David's battle with Goliath. David was too young to serve in Israel's army, which required a minimum age of twenty. So, David was probably between fifteen and nineteen years old when his father, Jesse, sent him to bring food to his three older brothers, who were serving in Israel's army. The Philistine champion, who was about nine-and-a-half feet tall, stepped out from the camp and, twice a day for forty days, taunted Israel's army by yelling, "Choose a man for yourselves and let him come down to me. If he is able to fight with me and strike me down, then we will become your slaves; but if I prevail against him and strike him down, then you shall become our slaves and serve us" (1 Samuel 17:8b–9). Israel's entire army was paralyzed with fear, and not one soldier stepped forward to fight Goliath.

But when David heard Goliath's challenge, he revealed his fearless heart as he asked, "For who is this uncircumcised Philistine, that he should reproach the battle lines of the living God?" (1 Samuel 17:26). After receiving Saul's approval to face Goliath, this young man, with no military training and no armor except a sling and five stones, went to confront the enemy of God's people. David was not afraid of this giant warrior (Psalm 34:4, 56:3–4). Nor was he impressed by his enemies' weapons, for he said, "You come to me with a sword, a spear, and a javelin, but I come to you in the name of Yahweh of hosts, the God of the battle lines of Israel, whom you have reproached" (1 Samuel 17:45). Take note that Goliath came with his weapons (things). In contrast, David went with the King of the universe (relationship). David was angry because this giant did not revere Almighty Yahweh. Even before the short battle, David honored Yahweh by predicting Goliath's defeat (1 Samuel 17:46). David used a small stone, and Goliath lost his big head. David had no fear of man, but he did fear (revere) Yahweh. The more your reverence for Yahweh increases, the less you will fear anyone or anything.

Three Types of Fear

Of the three types of fear, the first and most important is *positive fear*, which is the fear of God. This fear should be understood as reverence and awe for your Creator. In Proverbs 1:7, we are told, "The fear of Yahweh is the beginning of knowledge." In this context, the word *fear* is a noun (*yir'āh*), representing a positive fear to hold onto and cherish.

The second is the *natural fear* that everyone feels. When you see a large fin above the water while swimming, feeling scared is a normal reaction. For John Flavel,

> Such fear is an essential part of human nature (a key to survival), because we fear what threatens us, and in response, we avoid what we fear,[ii] Everyone experiences natural fear. It is the trouble or agitation of mind that arises when we perceive approaching evil or impending danger. It is not always sinful, but it is always the fruit and consequence of sin. Ever since sin entered human nature, it has been impossible to shake off this fear.[iii]

The third type of fear is *sinful fear*. According to John Flavel, "natural fear can quickly turn into sinful fear. That happens when fear springs from 'unbelief, and an unworthy distrust of God.' In other words, natural fear becomes sinful fear when we fail to trust God's promises in the face of danger."[iv]

Sinful fear is something you are meant to avoid and turn away from. We see both positive and sinful fear in Exodus 20:20: "And Moses said to the people, 'Do not be afraid; for God has come in order to test you, and so that the fear of Him may be with you, so that you may not sin.'" When Moses says, "Do not be afraid," he uses the verb (*yārē'*), which in this context refers to a negative fear that should be avoided. However, Moses also uses the noun for fear (yir'āh), which in context is a positive fear that God's people are meant to have for Him.

The negative fear, as shown in this chapter's heading verse (Isaiah 41:10), comes from fearing people, the world, or the devil, which leads to sin—all three try to turn you away from your loving, heavenly Father. However, in Exodus 20:20, God uses testing to guide His people back to fearing (revering) Him so they won't sin. Therefore, the more you fear Yahweh, the less negative fear you'll feel, and the less you will sin.

The positive form of fear is rooted in God's Word (Psalm 119:38; Proverbs 2:1–6) and helps open your mind to receive God's wisdom and knowledge (Proverbs 1:7, 9:10). Solomon states that the purpose of life is to fear (revere) God and keep His commandments (Ecclesiastes 12:13). However, sinful emotions such as bitterness and fear close your mind to wisdom and knowledge, diminishing the quality of intimacy and reverence for your heavenly Father (Ephesians 4:26–32).

A Misplaced Loyalty

Sinful fear shows misplaced loyalty. Return to God's truth, which leads to freedom. Fear or anxiety can't bring joy, but faith in Jesus' work for you can give eternal joy and satisfaction (Psalm 16:11). David's fear of Yahweh overshadowed any fear he had of Goliath. This is the fear in David's heart recorded in 1 Samuel 17:45: "Then David said to the Philistine, 'You come to me with a sword, a spear, and a javelin, but I come to you in the name of Yahweh of hosts, the God of the battle lines of Israel, whom you have reproached.'" In other words, reverence for Yahweh is the cure for any sinful fear.

Another instance of misplaced loyalty appears in Isaiah 30, when Sennacherib (Isaiah 36:1) and his mighty army prepare to invade Israel. God assures His people through the prophet Isaiah that they will be strengthened in "quietness and trust" (v. 15). They are told to depend on Yahweh rather than the Egyptians; however, they refuse.

Weak Christians fear man and circumstances, while strong Christians revere Yahweh. It's important to recognize that reverence is a choice. The weak follower of God is depicted in Isaiah 30, where Israel, fearing the Assyrians, sought help. Instead of trusting in Yahweh, they turned to Egypt (see Proverbs 3:5), which they were told never to do (Isaiah 31:1–3). Relying on Egypt was a form of bondage for the Jews, and we likewise become enslaved when trusting in anyone other than Yahweh.

If Christians are not vigilant, they can be influenced by the world to be afraid of things and people they can't control. I'm sure the fear of Israel's army was contagious and spread like a plague among the Jews as they stood in front of Goliath. But not so with David, who ran toward the enemy because he revered and trusted in Yahweh. You can do the same. It all depends on choosing to be enslaved by your fears or to live in freedom by revering Yahweh. When you face the Goliaths of the world, ask yourself, "Is there anyone or anything my loving, heavenly Father can't control or protect me from?" I encourage you to memorize and reflect on Isaiah 41:10. The prophet Isaiah is calling you to be strengthened by your relationship with the great I AM, rather than being paralyzed by any circumstance. We are called to live in God's truth because of Jesus' love (2 Corinthians 5:14–15) and his kindness toward us (Romans 2:4).

When you feel afraid, do you first assess your own strength or that of your friend, or do you immediately turn to your almighty Father God? When you trust God and set Him apart (make Him holy) in your mind and acknowledge that He is "other" than anyone or anything else regarding your current fear, He will lead you to peace (Romans 15:13).

Flavel adds some significant insights in the following:

It is a great sin to love or fear any creature above its worth, as if it were a master of all our temporal and eternal comforts. The sinfulness of our fear lies in its excessiveness. To fear something more than we ought is bad enough, but to magnify its power above that of a creature is sinful. When we exalt a creature's power by fearing it, we give it ascendancy over us. In effect, we act as if it had arbitrary and absolute dominion over us and our comforts—to do with them whatever it pleases. In so doing, we elevate the creature beyond its class and rank to the place of God. This is a very sinful and evil fear. To trust in any creature as if it had God's power to help us, or to fear any creature as if it had God's power to hurt us is exceedingly sinful. It provokes God.[v]

We learn Yahweh's perspective on this human tendency in Isaiah 51:12–13a: "I, even I, am He who comforts you. Who are you that you are afraid of man who dies and of the son of man who is made like grass, that you have forgotten Yahweh your Maker?" Flavel notes the following: "Be careful not to fear any man, as if the power of making or marring you were in his hands—as if it were his will and pleasure to save or ruin you . . . The sinfulness of fear consists in the distracting influence it has upon the heart, whereby it unfits us for the discharge of our duties."[vi]

Note how Jehoshaphat responded when fearful in 2 Chronicles 20:2–3: "Then some came and told Jehoshaphat, saying, 'A great multitude is coming against you from beyond the sea, out of Aram, and behold, they are in Hazazon-tamar (that is, Engedi).' And Jehoshaphat was afraid and set his face to seek Yahweh, and called for a fast throughout all Judah."

To live all day and night in the fear of man or in the trust of man is foolish and will bring you no freedom or relief (Deuteronomy 28:65–67; Proverbs 29:25). However, when you fear Yahweh, you will walk in righteousness, avoiding sin (Proverbs 16:6).

In the rest of this chapter, my goal is to provide clear and concise truth statements that you can focus on and perhaps meditate on for a minute or two.

How Can You Grow in Reverence of God?

Ask God to give you a strong sense of His reverence. Jeremiah 32:40: "And I will cut an everlasting covenant with them that I will not turn away from them, to do them good; and I will put the fear of Me in their hearts so that they will not turn away from Me."

Obedience leads to Jesus' revealing more of Himself to you (Proverbs 8:17; John 14:21). The more you know Him, the more you will revere Him. The more you revere Yahweh, the more you will trust and obey Him. "Trembling before man brings a snare, but he who trusts in Yahweh will be set securely on high" (Proverbs 29:25). When we doubt God's ability or willingness to intervene on our behalf, our faith weakens, and our fear of man grows (Proverbs 29:25).

Don't fear man more than God. Take note of how Moses responded to his circumstance in Hebrews 11:27: "By faith he left Egypt, not fearing the rage of the king; for he endured, as seeing Him who is unseen."

Denying yourself, picking up your cross, and following Jesus (Luke 9:23) will lead to greater reverence for your Savior. Notice what God told Abraham in Genesis 22:12: "And He said, 'Do not stretch out your hand against the boy, and do nothing to him; for now I know that you fear God, since you have not withheld your son, your only one, from Me.'"

Ask the Lord to increase your hatred of the sin within you so that you will turn from it. Job 1:1: "There was a man in the land of Uz whose name was Job; and that man was blameless, upright, fearing God, and turning away from evil."

Don't deny your God-given identity in Christ. There's no need for Christians to live in negative fear, knowing we live in a world controlled by the devil. Notice the two realities 1 John 5:19–20 shares: "We know that we are of God, and that the whole world lies in the power of the evil one. And we know that the Son of God has come, and has given us understanding so that we may know Him who is true; and we are in Him who is true, in His Son Jesus Christ. This is the true God and eternal life." John clearly affirms that believers live in a world under the influence of our evil adversary, but, more importantly, he teaches that we have a God-given understanding that enables us to know Jesus and be in Him, who is the Truth. Therefore, don't ignore the environment you live in; do not be surprised when harm occurs around you and to you. But also, don't deny your God-given identity in Christ. Yes, you are in enemy territory, but inside you (1 John 4:4) is the Great Warrior King of the universe, who has already defeated the devil. Therefore, live confidently in this great truth!

Considerations for Dealing with Your Fears

Set your entire life on His promise to work everything for good. Romans 8:28: "And we know that for those who love God all things work together for good, for those who are called according to His purpose."

Acknowledge that you are standing on Him right now. Psalm 92:15: "To declare that Yahweh is upright; He is my rock, and there is no unrighteousness in Him."

Remember, one day He will remove all of your troubles forever. Revelation 7:17: "For the Lamb at the center of the throne will shepherd them and will guide them to springs of the water of life. And God will wipe every tear from their eyes." Therefore, don't fix your eyes on your present problems but on His eternal blessings, because your present problems are temporary while God's promises are eternal (2 Corinthians 4:18; Romans 8:18).

When Paul compared his life and possessions to his reverence for Jesus, there was no comparison. We are told in Acts 20:24, "But I do not make my life of any account nor dear to myself, so that I may finish my course and the ministry which I received from the Lord Jesus, to testify solemnly of the gospel of the grace of God." How could Paul live this way? The answer is recorded in Revelation 12:11: "And they overcame him [the devil] because of the blood of the Lamb and because of the word of their witness, and they did not love their life even to death." The love of things, pleasures, comforts, and people are common reasons why we fear losing them, but the greatest reason we fear is because of our love of self. Overcoming these loves, including self-love, is an internal struggle that can be won only through a conviction that the Bible is the sole source of truth regarding God, life, salvation, and sanctification.

As I write this chapter, my wife and I are on a brief getaway to a hot spring in Colorado. In the locker room, I spoke with a Catholic priest. He asked if I was a Catholic, and I said no, but I had some questions. He was willing to respond, so I asked, "If I were to ask you right now how to have eternal life, what would you say?" He replied, "You would need to have faith in Jesus and do good works." I clarified, "Just to be sure, you said I need to have faith and do good works to become a Christian, correct?" He said, "Yes." I then asked him to help me understand how he views Ephesians 2:8–9 and Titus 3:5, which I quoted. I explained that both passages clearly state that works are unrelated to salvation and only faith is required. He responded, "When Jesus healed people, He said, 'Go, and sin no more.'" I was surprised because the context of that passage wasn't about salvation but about adherence to the old covenant law, which was still in effect, as Jesus had not yet gone to the cross. I agree that Jesus didn't want people to sin, but the four primary purposes of the law were first, to reveal that God has a perfect standard; second, to show that you can't keep it; third, to show that you have earned judgment; and fourth, to point to the Messiah as the only solution to your eternal problem. According to Romans 3:10–12, no one can earn salvation through good works, for no one is able to do good works apart from Christ in him (Romans 7). I then asked the priest how he deals with the fact that what he says about salvation contradicts God's Word. I told him that, according to the Bible, everything we need for life and godliness has already been given to us (2 Peter 1:3; 2 Timothy 3:16). What else do we need? He didn't try to address this contradiction but instead appealed to church tradition and the Pope. He then stated that he had to leave for a meeting, and our conversation concluded.

I tell this story to show how easy and common it is for any of us to turn away from the truth that is clearly documented in the Bible and turn to other authorities, solutions, or feelings that lead us to live in ways that contradict the truth. Trying to achieve salvation through faith and good works is another gospel, and according to Galatians 1:6–10, anyone who does so is cursed. In addition, for you or me to live by feelings rather than by truth is not the way our Lord wants us to live.

The verses at the top of this chapter tell us not to fear, for

God is with us. What should we do when we fear? Do we look for some other authority or feeling apart from God's Word to help us? If you do, you will not experience the freedom Jesus speaks of in John 8:31–32; instead, you will live in the bondage of any teaching or feelings that you choose to follow that is contrary to God's Word.

To overcome the focus of loving our lives on this fallen planet, we must have a greater love for the One who not only gives us physical and eternal life but is Life Himself (John 14:6). Loving your life at the expense of loving the Life is idolatry; therefore, we see why in Luke 14:26, Jesus tells His disciples, "If anyone comes to Me, and does not hate his own father and mother and wife and children and brothers and sisters, yes, and even his own life, he cannot be My disciple."

The fundamental question we must ask is, "Do I really believe God is sovereign and has, therefore, permitted these circumstances in my life that I am fearing?" To live above your fear is to have the conviction that God has not only permitted this situation but will work it out according to His will (Ephesians 1:11). I like how John MacArthur describes fear:

> Fear, by the way, is a liar . . . fear is a liar. Fear tells you tomorrow is something to be afraid of. Fear tells you you're not going to have what you need tomorrow. Fear tells you you're not going to be up to it. Fear tells you if certain things happen, you're never going to be able to survive it. Fear tells you that there's terrible pain out there. Fear is a liar for the Christian because there is no thing that you're ever going to go through, no trial, no temptation, that God will not provide sufficient grace to sustain you in.[vii]

How to Live Without Fear in the Present

Ask the Lord to cause you to desire Him above everyone and everything (Psalm 73:25). Putting oneself first above all else, including one's Creator and Savior, is common for the unbeliever. For without life, he could enjoy nothing of the earth, other people, or possessions. Therefore, the unbeliever reasons that if he is dead, he can't enjoy anything on earth, and since his possessions on earth are all he has, his life is of utmost importance. But not so with Christians, for we are told in Mark 8:36, "For what does it profit a man to gain the whole world, and forfeit his soul?" The nonbeliever has no idea of a soul after death, but this is the Christian's greatest hope: a promise of eternal life with Jesus. As you consider choosing to live this way, is God's Word a sufficient source of hope and security, or do you choose to believe the lie that worth and value are based on your possessions and physical life?

When fearful, ask the Spirit to reveal the lie you are believing (Isaiah 41:10). You are beyond the range of Satan's fiery darts when you abide in Jesus. Negative fear keeps you away from Jesus, while reverence for Him keeps you in intimate communion with Him.

Remember, your entire life on earth is lived amid a spiritual battle. We see that Paul's mental readiness and anticipation of suffering gave him courage for what was to come, as in Acts 21:13: "Then Paul answered, 'What are you doing, crying and breaking my heart? For I am ready not only to be bound, but even to die at Jerusalem for the name of the Lord Jesus.'" Paul knew the earth wasn't his permanent home; he chose to live as an alien on this planet, and so must we. Make the choice that, in comparison to eternity, you won't be here long. Therefore, take the next step in the race that God has set before you, keeping your eyes fixed on Jesus (Hebrews 12:1–2).

Surrendering to God's will is your first step. As you grow in faith, your willingness to surrender your will and life to God also grows. Consider King David's willing submission to the will of Yahweh, as he instructs Zadok, the high priest, in 2 Samuel 15:25–26: "Then the king said to Zadok, 'Return the ark of God to the city. If I find favor in the sight of Yahweh, then He will cause me to return and show me both it and His habitation. But if He should say thus, "I have no delight in you," behold, here I am, let Him do to me as seems good in His sight.'"

Remember, the devil tempts you to bring out your worst, while God tests you to bring out your best. Therefore, it is wise to view fear as a test of whether you trust Yahweh above all others. But you are told in 2 Peter 2:9, "The Lord knows how to rescue the godly from trial, and to keep the unrighteous under punishment for the day of judgment."

Choose to live in truth, not fear. A strong commitment to living in truth will enable you to trust even in difficult times. When you suddenly feel overwhelmed by fear, don't believe the lie that you have no options. You can choose to be overcome by fear or choose to surrender your life to Yahweh's will. Christian soldiers must not fall for the lie of self-preservation because they have already died to self (Galatians 2:20). Therefore, as a righteous soldier in Yahweh's army, live in His truth, not in your fear (Habakkuk 2:4; Romans 1:17; Galatians 3:11; Hebrews 10:38).

Do you want your Father's will to be done? Jesus could have summoned twelve legions of angels (Matthew 26:53), but he didn't. Why? Because he wanted his Father's will to be fulfilled. You might not be able to call down angels from heaven, but you can choose to believe the truth that your Abba has allowed obstacles, pain, and other challenges into your life. Like Joseph, you can declare that God intends this for good (Genesis 50:20; Romans 8:28). Therefore, your perspective, not your circumstances, can shift from anxiety or fear to firm, unwavering faith. The truth reveals that God uses these things to shape you into the image of Jesus. A biblical strategy for dealing with temporary and unwanted troubles is not to dwell on them. Consider Paul's strategy in 2 Corinthians 4:17–18 (NLT):

> For our present troubles are small and won't last very long. Yet they produce for us a glory that vastly outweighs them and will last forever! So we don't look at the troubles we can see now; rather, we fix our gaze on things that cannot be seen. For the things we see now will soon be gone, but the things we cannot see will last forever.

The freedom God intends requires you to see everything that comes your way as an opportunity to become more like Jesus. Pain, sorrow, and the loss of family and friends will happen, and you can't prevent them. However, you can choose to respond truthfully, trusting God will use these for good and shape you more into the image of Jesus (Hebrews 12:1–3).

Rest and commune with your Savior. The focus right now is not to change your feelings but to rest and commune with Jesus so you can glorify God even amid your negative feelings and circumstances. We don't glorify God by focusing on trouble but on the promises of God's truth—the things that last forever. This is how God is glorified in whatever happens in your life (1 Corinthians 10:31).

The principle is that suffering (your cross) comes before glory. The name of our home church is Cross and Crown. The idea is that you carry your cross on earth before you receive your crown in heaven. This is a good perspective to keep throughout your sanctification. This was true in Jesus' life, and it still holds true for us today (Luke 24:26; Hebrews 2:10).

Consider the freedom expressed in the following statement: Growth in glory always involves denying oneself and trusting God, even when one is unsure of what He is doing (Proverbs 3:5–6).

Promises to Claim When You Are Fearful

God's desire to protect you comes from His love for you. Psalm 91:14–15: "Because he has loved Me, therefore I will protect him; I will set him securely on high, because he has known My name. He will call upon Me, and I will answer him; I will be with him in his distress; I will rescue him and honor him."

God Almighty is on your side; this truth should give you the courage to march forward in your battle with fear. Hebrews 13:5b: "For He Himself has said, 'I will never desert you, nor will I ever forsake you.'"

You must remember that your God not only loves you but is good, and, therefore, He will never do anything that is not best for you. Psalm 118:6: "Yahweh is for me; I will not fear; what can man do to me?" This doesn't mean your Abba won't allow difficult circumstances in your life, but they won't last forever, and He will be with you through them.

The positive fear in Jeremiah 32:40 attests to God's good intentions toward His followers. Jeremiah 32:40: "And I will cut an everlasting covenant with them that I will not turn away from them, to do them good; and I will put the fear of Me in their hearts so that they will not turn away from Me." The word *fear* is not synonymous with "reverence," but rather a positive fear of God (Exodus 20:20). This is the same fear that motivated and delighted Jesus, as described in Isaiah 11:2–3. This type of fear is rooted in God's Word (Psalm 119:38; Proverbs 2:1–5) and can eliminate all other fears. Don't forget that God is always with you, even when you can't sense His presence (Hebrews 13:5).

Currently, my good friend Phil's life seems to be in the hands of the prison system, but he knows his God loves him and is in sovereign control of his life. Psalm 31:15: "My times are in Your hand; deliver me from the hand of my enemies and from those who pursue me."

Are you willing to step aside and surrender to the will of the One who created you for Himself? Luke 22:42: "Father, if You are willing, remove this cup from Me, yet not My will, but Yours be done."

Don't Forget To . . .

Regularly renew your mind (chapter three). Your biggest enemy isn't the devil but the lies you believe about yourself, especially when they become your strongest inclinations.

Stay cautious. You might feel safe and secure at home, but stay cautious. There may come a time, like with my close friend Phil, when your home feels more like a prison cell. At that point, you'll need a source of security that far surpasses what this world can offer.

Put on the armor of God daily. Hughes, a Christian counselor, suggests that "some may not put on God's armor because of ignorance, neglect, complacency, or despair." Another reason may be arrogance. I wonder whether or not wearing God's armor means you believe you can handle whatever the world, flesh, and devil throw at you each day. This is not only a lie but also foolish and prideful thinking. Regardless of the reasons, putting on the armor of God is a choice available to every Christian. The apostle Paul commands in Ephesians 6:11, "Put on the full armor of God, so that you will be able to stand firm against the schemes of the devil." This command is grounded in the foundational truths recorded in Ephesians 1–3. Truth is something Christians can choose, and that choice is fostered through a deepening relationship of love with Jesus (John 14:21).

Avoid the sand. Keep in mind that there are only two options in Matthew 7:24–27. You either choose to rest your life on your sand or on the Rock of your salvation (Psalm 89:26). Again, you will select your strongest inclination. However, you can't choose both because any faith in yourself is like trusting quicksand, since the man who depends on himself has nothing to rely on except the breath in his nostrils (Isaiah 2:22).

Remember, feelings are not enduring. Feelings alone will never be enough to help you endure the trials, sorrows, and suffering of this world. But accepting the unconditional love of Jesus and the joy and glory that await you will give you the strength to persevere.

Your Death Is Getting Closer

There is great peace when you know that your all-powerful, all-knowing, and ever-present Sovereign God of the universe controls everything that happens, including your death. Therefore, since He loves you and is good, you can choose to rest in His will, even regarding your death.

When I was a child and felt scared, I ran to my dad or mom. No one loved me as they did, and they were both stronger and wiser than I was. So, as an adult with many weaknesses, is there anyone better to run to than your Abba (Isaiah 63:16)? Since you have already been promised eternal life by Him (2 Timothy 1:12), surely you can trust Him with your physical life. Don't forget, apart from being raptured, you are going to die. But Christians are victors and aren't to fear death, for it is no longer victorious over us (1 Corinthians 15:54–55). Jesus defeated death by rising from the grave. The sting of death is sin, and the power of sin is the law (1 Corinthians 15:55–57), but Jesus' crucifixion paid the penalty for our sins, thereby satisfying the law on behalf of all His followers (Romans 6:23). Therefore, what do Christians have to fear about death? The results of your physical death are the completion of your practical holiness and your entrance into the presence of the Holy Trinity for eternity.

While on earth, all Christians will never be completely free from the sins within us or the influence of the world and Satan from outside, including the negative feelings that come with them. But even though we know we will die, the devil can no longer hold our sins or the fear of death over us because we are permanently in Jesus (Romans 7:24–25). Therefore, we understand that when we die physically, it will happen at God's perfectly appointed time and in His perfect way. Furthermore, all our concerns, relationships, possessions, and negative feelings will no longer matter. But best of all, when you open your eyes, you will see Jesus and be like Him forever (1 John 3:2).

Freedom, Not Fear

God's ways are not your ways (Isaiah 55:8), and He wants you to live in the peace He has already given you (John 14:27). Therefore, reject the lie that life must go your way—this is bondage. Remember, freedom isn't about doing whatever you want. True freedom is the ability to express and genuinely believe that your life will unfold according to God's plan (Philippians 1:6).

There is a difference between knowing you can't watch the championship game and being unable to prevent the death of a spouse, family member, friend, or your own death. Yet, each situation comes from the same sovereign, loving, and good God who created you for Himself, not for yourself. His ways will always lead to greater glory and freedom, just as He planned for you before He made you.

———

I encourage you to listen to "Fear is a Liar" by Zack Williams (2016) and "No Fear" by Jon Reddick (2025).

Small-group Discussion Questions

1. Is there any fear that could enter your life over which God is not sovereign? Explain.

2. How does fear serve as a form of bondage?

3. Describe a recent fear you experienced. What were you afraid of? Was it the loss of something, someone, your health, or your life? Whatever it was, was it a temporary loss or an eternal one? Explain the difference.

Suggestions for Freedom from Fear

1. When fearful, ask the Spirit to show you the lie you are believing (Isaiah 41:10). You are out of the range of Satan's fiery darts when you abide in Jesus. Fear can keep you away from Jesus, while revering Him keeps you in intimate communion.

2. Remember, suffering comes before glory. The glory you will receive is more certain than your current fear. Therefore, like Stephen (Acts 7:55–56), look up to heaven, remembering that no matter what happens, you have been promised to be with Jesus forever.

3. It is your strong commitment to live in truth that enables you to trust even in difficult times. When you suddenly feel overwhelmed by fear, don't believe the lie that you have no options. You can choose to be overcome by fear or choose to surrender your life to Yahweh's will. The Christian soldier must not fall for the lie of self-preservation because you already died to self (Galatians 2:20). Therefore, since you are a righteous soldier in Yahweh's army, you should walk by faith, not by fear (Habakkuk 2:4; Romans 1:17; Galatians 3:11; Hebrews 10:38).

Chapter Eight

FREEDOM FROM UNRIGHTEOUS ANGER

*Be angry, and yet do not sin; do not let the sun go down
on your anger, and do not give the devil an opportunity.*
EPHESIANS 4:26–27

The Commonality of Anger

It's difficult to watch the nightly news without seeing some form of anger. Either news commentators are upset about an event that has occurred, or they're angry about something that "should have happened" but didn't. Often, anger is expressed by those being interviewed, who are frustrated over what they have lost due to crimes, flooding, hurricanes, or the death of a loved one. Of course, if sin didn't exist, there would be no anger, but that doesn't mean all anger is sinful. In fact, there is a need for righteous anger worldwide. Still, for Christians, it can be challenging to feel anger without sinning (Ephesians 4:26). Throughout the Gospels, Jesus often expressed anger (Matthew 23:13–36). Still, it was always righteous and justified in response to those with whom He spoke. As Christians, Jesus is our example of how to think, speak, and act. Although we are justified in Christ and stand before God as holy and righteous by virtue of our position in Him, we often struggle to live out our positional holiness in daily life, particularly in managing anger. Yes, Christians have been set free from their previous slavery to sin, but the presence of sin, including unrighteous anger, can still surface in us and may appear quickly if we are not led by the Holy Spirit (Galatians 5:16–23).

As you learned in chapter two, your behavior—including anger—is expressed either righteously or unrighteously based on your strongest inclinations. The key to developing righteous inclinations was discussed in chapter three, where you learned that renewing your mind with the truth of Scripture is a necessary daily activity in your transformation process. This is reflected in the heading verse of this chapter (Ephesians 4:26–27) and in the command of James 1:19–20: "Know this, my beloved brothers. But everyone must be quick to hear, slow to speak, and slow to anger; for the anger of man does not achieve the righteousness of God." Both of these references clearly indicate that anger is a choice (Colossians 3:8). Furthermore, choosing unrighteous anger exposes the lie that "other people make me angry!" No! Every time you become angry, it is due to your greatest inclination, which you chose to act upon. In contrast, righteous anger is cultivated through a deliberate choice to listen carefully to the person speaking and to the Holy Spirit, followed by a slow-to-speak approach.

All Christians should remember that Scripture is truth (John 17:17), while feelings are not. Feelings can deceive us and keep us from living in the truth. However, feelings rooted in truth are both God-honoring and conducive to experiencing God's freedom. For Scripture to become your strongest inclination, the verses in your mind must shift from knowledge to conviction (1 Corinthians 8:1). This is why renewing your mind is so valuable and necessary, as it identifies the lies in your mind and replaces them with God's truth.

The Blazing Furnace or God's Blazing Glory

There may be many Bible verses stored in your mind that you don't fully believe. Words in your mind are just knowledge, but when they move to your heart, they are lived out in practical application. The conviction of that knowledge is evident in the way you speak and act, unlike mere facts stagnating in your head. The process of biblical truth moving to conviction includes God-honoring behavior and feelings (Luke 24:32). These demonstrate that God's Word is more than mere knowledge and provide evidence of one's love for Jesus (John 14:21).

Consider what may have been going through the minds of Shadrach, Meshach, and Abed-nego in Daniel 3. They were commanded by the king to bow to his idol or be thrown into the blazing furnace. If they had chosen a self-centered perspective, they would have done whatever was necessary to avoid the furnace, knowing the fire would consume them. But these young, godly men chose a God-centered perspective. Although they were confident God could save them, they still acknowledged they might be thrown into the furnace. But it didn't matter, because God's glory outweighed their inclination to self-preservation. In Daniel 3:16–18, after the king ordered them to bow to his idol, we see these young men's God-centered response:

> Shadrach, Meshach, and Abed-nego answered and said to the king, "O Nebuchadnezzar, we do not need to respond to you with an answer concerning this matter. If it be so, our God whom we serve is able to save us from the furnace of blazing fire; and He will save us out of your hand, O king. But if not, let it be known to you, O king, that we are not going to serve your gods, and we will not worship the golden image that you have set up."

The above response elicited anger from the king toward these young men; however, observe the change in the king's perspective after these men were thrown into the furnace (Daniel 3:24–25, 28–30):

> Then Nebuchadnezzar the king was astounded and hurriedly stood up; he answered and said to his high officials, "Was it not three men we cast tied up into the midst of the fire?" They answered and said to the king, "Certainly, O king." He answered and said, "Look! I see four men loosed and walking about in the midst of the fire without harm, and the appearance of the fourth is like a son of the gods!" . . . Nebuchadnezzar answered and said, "Blessed be the God of Shadrach, Meshach, and Abed-nego, who has sent His angel and saved His servants who put their trust in Him, violating the king's word, and gave up their bodies so as not to serve and not to worship any god except their own God. Therefore I make a decree that any people, nation, or tongue that says

anything offensive against the God of Shadrach, Meshach, and Abed-nego shall be torn limb from limb and their houses reduced to a rubbish heap, inasmuch as there is no other god who is able to deliver in this way." Then the king caused Shadrach, Meshach, and Abed-nego to succeed in the province of Babylon.

The king's perspective shifted from his own impotent god, whom he demanded Shadrach, Meshach, and Abed-nego bow to. When they refused, he became angry. But when the king saw what happened in the furnace, his unrighteous anger fell, and he turned his focus away from his impotent idol. His anger turned to reverence and awe, and his meaningless idol crumbled before the blazing glory of Yahweh.

Can you see Shadrach, Meshach, and Abed-nego's self-denial and willingness to die bringing blazing glory to Yahweh? If these three men had chosen to live by their feelings, none of this would have happened. But they trusted God by choosing to obey His Word, and Yahweh received blazing glory from the king and his high officials.

These men knew the truths of the first and second commandments: "You shall have no other gods before [Yahweh]" (Exodus 20:3) and you must avoid idol worship (see Exodus 20:4–5). They chose to obey because they were here on earth to bring their God glory, even if it meant their deaths.

The God-centered perspective of these three men will grow within you as you are sanctified. But it can't grow if you are not renewing your mind with truth and meditating on it to guard the inclinations of your mind (Psalm 119:9, 11; Joshua 1:8). Since the only way to please God is by faith (Hebrews 11:6), we must expect that God will regularly give us opportunities to grow in faith by choosing to live in the freedom of His truth.

How Can You Develop Conviction About the Truth of God in Your Mind?

The apostle Paul tells believers in 1 Thessalonians 1:5, "For our gospel did not come to you in word only, but also in power and in the Holy Spirit and with full assurance [conviction]; just as you know what kind of men we proved to be among you for your sake." Paul assured the

Thessalonians that the Word of God he preached was more than just words. It came with power, in the Holy Spirit, and with full conviction. Specifically, Paul was referring to the gospel he first heard and shared with the Thessalonians. If God's power doesn't accompany His Word in your response to others, it will be just words and won't make an impact on the listener. The listener will only be a hearer, not a doer (James 1:22–25). Whether you're sharing the gospel or teaching another part of God's Word, it will only be words if you don't rely on the Spirit to empower you to speak and to use your words to open listeners' minds.

Developing conviction requires more than just storing God's Word in your brain. Consider Psalm 119:9: "How can a young man keep his way pure? By keeping it according to Your word" and Psalm 119:11: "Your word I have treasured in my heart, that I may not sin against You." The keyword in verse 9 is *keeping* (guarding), which shows conviction—turning knowledge into action. Psalm 141:3 uses a different Hebrew word for "guard," conveying careful watchfulness aimed at prevention. The psalmist of 119 is a godly man, but he is deeply aware of his lack of perfection.

Avoiding unrighteous anger requires not only having God's Word in your mind but also living in it. In other words, you guard your life with the sword of God's Word. H. C. Leupold asks us to "note throughout [the psalm] how the law is sought for the very purpose of being kept, not for the sake of attaining a theoretical knowledge of it."[i]

The idea of "putting into practice" is emphasized in the first eight verses of Psalm 119 through terms such as *walk, observe, seek, keep,* and *learn.* These verbs guide us from awareness to action. I appreciate that God chose to use people throughout the Scriptures who had not yet attained sinlessness, as the apostle Paul states in Philippians 3:12, where he writes that he has not yet attained spiritual perfection. Your transformation is a journey, a race, beginning at your conversion and ending in complete perfection at your death or the rapture (Philippians 1:6). Paul also tells us that we are running in a race. According to 1 Corinthians 9:24–27,

> Do you not know that those who run in a race all run, but only one receives the prize? Run in such a way that you may win. Now everyone who competes in the games exercises self-control in all things. They then do it to receive a corruptible crown, but we an incorruptible.

Therefore I run in such a way, as not without aim; I box in such a way, as not beating the air; but I discipline my body and make it my slave, so that, after I have preached to others, I myself will not be disqualified.

When we finish our race, temptation and sin will be over forever. But we know that our race continues to reveal our weaknesses, our impulses to sin, and our tendencies toward self-centeredness. Yet these are never to be used as an excuse. I have heard so many people say, "Well, I'm only human," as if that was an excuse to sin. The apostle Paul, in Romans 7:15–25, says he wants to do good but falls short on his own. He recognizes that his ability to obey comes through Christ Jesus. This truth is also echoed by the psalmist in 119:5: "Oh may my ways be established to keep Your statutes!" This isn't only true for the psalmist and the apostle Paul, but also for you. Only God can establish your ways according to His Word. Here, we find the biblical root of Augustine's prayer, "Oh God, grant what thou dost command and command what thou dost desire."

We learn that wanting to do the Word of God, which is common among Christians, differs from actually doing it. Doing it requires reliance on the Holy Spirit and His power. Let's revisit 1 Thessalonians 1:5: "For our gospel did not come to you in word only, but also in power and in the Holy Spirit and with full assurance." When someone truly accepts the Word of God, the Holy Spirit and His power are active. Without the Spirit and His power, all that exists are words. This is why when nonbelievers hear God's Word but don't believe, they are unable to understand or be changed because the Holy Spirit and His power haven't come upon them (1 Peter 1:23–25; 1 Corinthians 4:20; Ephesians 2:4–5).

Although 1 Thessalonians 1:5 explicitly mentions the gospel, the saints of old—the psalmists, Paul, and Augustine—affirm that God's Spirit and power are necessary to live out the truth that the Spirit has inscribed on the heart (Jeremiah 31:33; Hebrews 10:16). The apostle Paul knew the Thessalonians' preaching included the Spirit's power because it was full of conviction (certain persuasion). Just as the Spirit empowered the apostles to proclaim God's Word, that same power is needed to obey God's Word; this is how conviction is experienced. Paul tells us in Galatians 5:16, "Walk by the Spirit and you will not carry out the desire of the flesh." In other words, if you walk by the Spirit, you will not express unrighteous anger. Ephesians 4:26 instructs us, "Be angry, and yet do not sin; do not let the sun go down on your anger." Just as relying on your own ability to keep the law will never lead to salvation, neither can you avoid unrighteous anger on your own (Galatians 3:22). The best you can do on your own is to become a modern-day Pharisee, who outwardly appears righteous but inwardly is lawless (Matthew 23:28).

As a Christian, if you could obey God's Word from your heart without the Holy Spirit, you wouldn't need Him for your sanctification. Just as we know salvation is in Christ alone, we must also understand sanctification is a joint effort with the Spirit working within us. This is where the power and ability come from to avoid unrighteous anger and to display the fruit of the Holy Spirit.

There are two truths I am trying to convey. First, developing conviction about unrighteous anger requires more than a determined will and slow tongue. Second, to avoid unrighteous anger, listen carefully to what the other person is saying and resist the urge to react immediately. Steve Street wisely distinguishes between reacting and responding. "Reacting is automatic, while responding is thoughtful and intentional."

Therefore, while listening, avoid forming a reply in your mind, as it can block your understanding of what is being said. Instead, trust God to give you what He wants you to say once the person has finished speaking. This biblical approach (James 1:19) helps you better understand what is being communicated and gives you time to hear and reflect on what God gives you when He chooses to. In other words, during a conversation, you are not just engaged in a dialogue but in a "trialogue." The person is speaking, you are listening, and you are waiting on the Spirit's help. The truth the Spirit has for you to share will come from Him as you listen carefully and remain slow to speak (James 1:19). This wise approach to conversation will not only allow wisdom to flow easily from your lips (responding) but also help prevent unrighteous anger (reacting). Furthermore, you will be imitating Yahweh (Numbers 14:18).

In a heated exchange, our reactions are often impulsive and can lead to sorrow and regret. Responding, however, involves waiting and listening to the Holy Spirit, resulting in wisdom.

Know Thyself

In 1999, the film *The Matrix* was released, starring Keanu Reeves as Thomas Anderson, also known as Neo, a secret hacker and computer programmer. In this science fiction action movie, Neo discovers he has been living in a simulated reality since birth. The movie follows Neo as he tries to defeat the "feeling programs" that guard the Matrix. At one point, Neo visits the Oracle, a wise woman who helps him understand his true identity. When Neo enters the Oracle's kitchen, he sees above the doorway the Latin phrase *temet nosce,* meaning "know thyself." The Oracle helps him fulfill his key role in the story. It's important to note that Neo's identity is not revealed through his feelings but through the truth of who he truly is. In principle, this is true of every Christian. To have a proper understanding of yourself, you must not rely on your own understanding (Proverbs 3:5).

When you ask the Spirit for help, expect Him to answer your prayer. He may have you follow the wisdom of Jeremiah in Lamentations 3:40: "Let us search out and examine our ways, and let us return to Yahweh." One way to do this is by asking the Holy Spirit, "Why do I get so angry?" specifically, "Why was I so angry at ___?" When you ask questions like this, don't be in a hurry; listen quietly, and when an answer comes, compare it to what Scripture says. Fundamentally, you are asking the Spirit of God to give you wisdom about yourself. This is a good thing to do (James 1:5) and a pattern of renewing your mind. Patiently wait for the Spirit's guidance, for He will provide it, and according to James 3:17, it will have the following characteristics: "But the wisdom from above is first pure, then peaceable, considerate, submissive, full of mercy and good fruits, without doubting, without hypocrisy." He could respond immediately or within a few days. No matter when He replies, stay alert and anticipate His response, for He will gently provide the wisdom you've asked for.

Follow the humble heart of the psalmist in Psalm 139:23–24: "Search me, O God, and know my heart; try me and know my anxious thoughts; and see if there be any hurtful way in me, and lead me in the everlasting way." When the Spirit reveals the root cause or wrong inclination of your anger, the first step is to confess your sins to God (1 John 1:9) and, in humility, submit yourself to God (James 4:6–8). Submission requires humility and a willingness to ask the Lord to do with your life whatever He desires. After all, He not only made you but also created you for Himself (Colossians 1:16).

Understanding your identity in Christ is essential for both salvation and sanctification. A clear understanding of being created in God's image and being His adopted child allows you to relate properly to Him, yourself, others, and all of creation. Accurate self-awareness helps you make wise decisions and respond correctly to the sin within you in a way that honors your Creator and Savior. Growing in genuine self-knowledge is vital to spiritual growth and maturity. Understanding how God made you—including your strengths, weaknesses, impulses, needs, tendencies, talents, and spiritual gifts—provides more ways to glorify God here on earth. Self-knowledge is closely connected to avoiding self-deception, which the Bible warns against (James 1:22–24; Galatians 6:3; 1 Corinthians 3:18; 1 John 1:8). Knowing yourself enables you to be a better steward of what God has blessed you with, both naturally and spiritually.

Furthermore, wisdom involves knowing yourself, as we are told in Proverbs 14:8: "The wisdom of the prudent is to understand his way, but the folly of fools is deceit." Be a diligent student of yourself; however, be cautious not to rely solely on your own judgment of your problems or inclinations. For we are told in Proverbs 16:25, "There is a way which seems right to a man, but its end is the way of death." Most importantly, self-knowledge—having a biblical understanding of yourself—fosters genuine humility, enabling you to experience deeper communion with Jesus and grow in practical holiness.

Discernment and Slowness: A Wise Pairing

The primary Hebrew term for *discernment* in the Old Testament is *bin*, and its derivatives occur 247 times. It can mean "to understand," "to discern," or "to distinguish." Discernment is also common in the book of Proverbs, with its variants appearing at least twenty-one times. Proverbs 14:29 says, "He who is slow to anger has great discernment, but he who is quick-tempered raises up folly." Here, we see the importance of discernment in controlling your anger. This proverb highlights that patience demonstrates discernment and understanding, whereas a quick temper demonstrates impatience and foolishness. In this context, the purpose of discernment is to help individuals be slow to anger. Quick-tempered people are considered foolish because they are quick to speak and slow to listen, which often leads to trouble. If you live by the truth of this verse, you will enjoy healthy relationships and peace in your life. As Sid Buzzell said, "Controlling one's temper is always wise, and losing it is never wise!"

Slowness isn't a trait that often gets attention in sports, but it sparkles like a diamond in relationships, especially during conflict. Being quick-tempered is a common trait on Earth, regardless of race, gender, age, or religion. The truth of being slow to anger reveals great humility and discernment (understanding) and has interesting expressions in some languages; for example, "sits on his hot heart," "makes quiet his liver," "keeps his innermost silent," or "doesn't get hot inside quickly." Great understanding means to "have good sense," "be very wise," "show great intelligence or insight."[ii]

To understand how "slow to anger" is understood in Hebrew, we gain insight from Moses receiving the law on Mt. Sinai. We learn an interesting attribute of Yahweh in Exodus 34:6–7: "Then Yahweh passed by in front of him and called out, 'Yahweh, Yahweh God, compassionate and gracious, *slow to anger*, and abounding in lovingkindness and truth'" (emphasis added). In Hebrew, the word *anger* (*ap*) means "nose" and "nostril." Having a long nose is associated with being slow to anger, whereas having a short nose is associated with being quick-tempered (Proverbs 14:29).[iii] Theologically, God's long nose symbolizes His patience, mercy, and slowness to anger toward you.

In other words, if you have a long nose, you will be like Yahweh—patient, discerning, and slow to anger. According to Ecclesiastes 7:9, to be quick-tempered is to be a fool. Therefore, there is no shame but great wisdom in crying out to your heavenly Father and asking for a really long nose! Studying God's Word and praying over it regarding your unrighteous anger will produce the fruit of the Spirit, which includes self-control, and will help you become more like your holy Savior. Another way to view your spiritual journey is to consider whether your strongest inclination is to seek God's glory or your own.

John Cassian wisely referenced Proverbs 16:32 by saying,

> Everyone knows that patience is derived from passion and endurance and therefore that you cannot call anyone patient unless he endures indignities without annoyance. So Solomon rightly praised the patient

person: "Better is the patient man than the strong, and he who restrains his anger more than he that takes a city," and "A long-suffering man is mighty in prudence, but a fainthearted man is very foolish." Therefore, if a wronged man flares up in anger, the wrongful abuse should not be thought of as the cause of his sin but the manifestation of a *hidden weakness* (emphasis added). [iv]

Dr. Jeremy Pierre writes the following insights:

We need humble discernment into our own hearts to understand our anger. This discernment is a gift of the Holy Spirit that we must seek.

Discernment is the ability to make distinctions, to tell the difference between right and wrong, fitting and unfitting, beautiful and repulsive. In other words, your heart is turned to sense the difference between what is pleasing and displeasing to the Lord (Romans 12:1–2; Philippians 1:9–11). [v]

Often, unrighteous anger stems from the fear of losing something vital to your life. It might be your reputation, a possession, a relationship, a perceived need you believe is essential, or even the threat of losing your life. When you explore the greatest inclination of your unrighteous anger, turn in the New Testament to the book of James, known for its wisdom. James 4:1–4 offers a strong starting point for identifying inclinations of unrighteous anger:

What is the source of quarrels and conflicts among you? Is not the source your pleasures that wage war in your members? You lust and do not have, so you murder. You are envious and cannot obtain, so you fight and quarrel. You do not have because you do not ask. You ask and do not receive, because you ask with wrong motives, so that you may spend it on your pleasures. You adulteresses, do you not know that friendship with the world is enmity toward God? Therefore, whoever wishes to be a friend of the world sets himself as an enemy of God.

This passage not only offers insight into what you should look for in your life, but more importantly, what you can ask the Holy Spirit to remove from you. To consider some practical steps based on the wisdom of these verses, you could ask yourself the following questions when you experience an outburst of anger: First, was my sinful anger rooted in my pursuit of pleasure? Second, did my anger stem from a form of lust?

Third, is my anger rooted in envious thoughts toward someone? Fourth, has my sin come from wrongful motivations? Fifth, is my anger due to my desire to honor my God and King, or is it rooted in my love for myself?

A helpful song to listen to is "Angry Words"
by Horatio Richmond Palmer (1867).

Small-group Discussion Questions

1. Explain why knowing yourself—both the good and evil— is important.

2. What are the benefits of identifying the root cause of your anger?

3. James 4:1–4 highlights five underlying causes of anger: pleasures, lust, envy, wrong motives, and friendship with the world. Can you identify any other root causes of your anger?

Suggestions for Freedom from Anger

1. Each morning, pray through James 1:19–20: "Know this, my beloved brothers. But everyone must be quick to hear, slow to speak, and slow to anger; for the anger of man does not achieve the righteousness of God." Then, ask the Lord to make this true of you today.

2. Are you being threatened by someone or something? If so, does it matter that this threat isn't greater than God?

3. What changes could be made to remove your anger? If those changes happened, would it genuinely honor Jesus?

Chapter Nine

FREEDOM FROM LONELINESS

I lie awake, I have become like a lonely bird on a roof.
PSALM 102:7

An Only Child

I was adopted at age three and grew up in rural eastern Pennsylvania. My adoptive parents, Frank and Laura, whom I have always considered my real parents, loved me deeply. My dad was a service station owner and operator. I thought it was very fitting that he owned Sabo's Sunoco *Service* Station—very descriptive and fitting for my dad.

About a year before my parents died, I read Calvin Miller's book titled *The Table of Inwardness*. Even though it was out of print, it was an excellent resource for nurturing my intimacy with Christ. Chapter one is titled "The Issue of Inwardness." In this insightful chapter, Miller notes, "Inwardness is the place where the believer and his Lord meet."[i] He then identifies three paradoxes. I want to briefly examine his first paradox, as it relates to loneliness. He calls it "the aloneness-is-presence paradox."[ii]

Miller continues with the following: "Inwardness seeks someone to preside over the clean and the quiet. When Christ comes in, we have provided ourselves with an inner worship that is proper. We are not alone with quietness but with him. Inwardness is a reigning presence, and a quiet friend—a person, not a concept. The world may regard this as loneliness. But the paradox is set; aloneness is the presence."[iii]

I pondered this paradox for a long time and felt I had a good understanding of its meaning. Not long after, my dad passed away from congestive heart failure. I was living with my wife and four children 700 miles away in Illinois. Though I wanted to bring my mom to Illinois, she preferred to die in the home where I grew up. So, I hired three caring women from hospice, who looked after my mom during three eight-hour shifts each day. I called every day to talk to her, and every three weeks, I traveled back to relieve the caregivers and look after my mom from Friday until I left for home on Sunday. On two occasions, I received calls saying my mom was dying and I needed to return quickly to Pennsylvania. Both times, I went, and my mom recovered, so I went back home. But when the third call came, I returned to my childhood home, and within a couple of hours, while sitting beside my mom, I watched and listened as she took her last breath, dying from the same heart disease that took my dad six months earlier.

The caregiver stayed with me as the mortician carried my mother's body out of our home. But soon the caregiver left, and then, as an only child with my wife and four children 700 miles west, I felt an avalanche of loneliness topple over me. I'm not sure what time I woke up the next morning, but when I remembered where I was and what had happened the night before, I was overwhelmed by the sorrow and loss of my parents. These loving people were once strangers who traveled to Philadelphia to Lutheran Children's Services and chose me from among other orphans to be their son. Since then, I have often reflected on being both chosen and adopted twice—once by my heavenly Father and once by my adoptive parents.

A Lonely Walk

As I slowly walked around the house where I grew up, I was surprised to hear the birds chirping and to easily recognize the sound of the local grain mill. Didn't they know my parents were gone? Didn't they realize my life had changed forever? In some ways, everything was the same, but in others, it was very different. The biggest difference was that I was completely alone. I *felt* so alone. This wasn't the first time I'd been alone in the home I grew up in, but it was the first time I'd been alone in this house since my parents had gone to heaven. During my slow, sorrowful walks through the two-story home, I recalled Calvin Miller's aloneness-is-presence paradox, but now I had a very different understanding of his insightful paradox. I was not only alone from people—I was alone with Jesus. A song (and video) that beautifully portrays this paradox is titled "Alone, Yet Not Alone" by Joni Eareckson Tada (2014).

I gradually came to understand the truth that being physically alone didn't mean I was truly alone. As I walked through the valley of the shadow of death, I experienced Jesus in a way I had never known Him before. Yes, even though I was alone, I was not lonely. For more than twenty days, I emptied and cleaned my parents' house. My wife kindly returned and spent a week with me, helping manage all the details. She is a professional Christian counselor and truly supported me in many ways to keep going. But she soon needed to return home to her other responsibilities as a mother and counselor. I was quickly reminded that I was alone, but Jesus was with me.

In his scholarly yet notably practical commentaries on the book of Psalms, James Montgomery Boice notes the following:

> Few things in life are worse than being in trouble and being entirely alone. Yet when things go wrong for us, when life turns sour, or when we are in serious trouble, we almost always have to go through it by ourselves. Alexander Maclaren wrote, "The soul that has to wade through deep waters has always to do it alone; for no human sympathy reaches to full knowledge of, or share in, even the best loved one's grief. We have companions in joy; sorrow we have to face by ourselves." Yet Maclaren adds, still speaking of the dark side of things but pointing upward to our hope, "Unless we have Jesus with us in the darkness, we have no one." [iv]

Ella Wheeler Wilcox (1855–1919), an American poet, wrote, "Laugh and the world laughs with you; Weep and you weep alone." [v]

Boice continues, "Christians find that although others may desert us in our troubles, we are never deserted by Jesus, who knows us thoroughly, understands all we are going through, and supports us in it." [vi]

A Lonely Cave

During David's flight into the wilderness from Saul, he had no food, nowhere to run, and no one to help him. He was alone and eventually hid in the cave of Adullam. In his early months of cave dwelling, before gathering his army of distressed men around him, he wrote Psalm 57 and 142. We see David's desperation and isolation in Psalm 142. In this psalm, we have an opportunity to enter into David's loneliness:

> With my voice to Yahweh, I cry aloud; with my voice to Yahweh, I make supplication. I pour out my complaint before Him; I declare my distress before Him. When my spirit was faint within me, You knew my path. In the way where I walk they have hidden a trap for me. Look to the right and see; that there is no one who regards me; a way of escape has been destroyed from me; no one cares for my soul. I cried out to You, O Yahweh; I said, "You are my refuge, my portion in the land of the living. Give heed to my cry of lamentation, for I am brought very low; deliver me from my persecutors, for they are too strong for me. Bring my soul out of prison, to give thanks to Your name; the righteous will encircle me, for You will deal bountifully with me."

David was not defeated, because his faith in Yahweh gave him hope —a hope that didn't let him down (Romans 5:3–5; 8:28). David surrendered, and so should you. Surrender is the last thing we are taught to do in physical war, but it is the first choice to make in spiritual warfare—not to your enemy but to your Commander-in-Chief, the One who has already won the war.

I believe that during David's solitude and desperation, he cried out loudly to Yahweh for help. He was in trouble, he knew it, and he was completely alone. I understand what that feels like. Before my parents died, I never once cried out to my heavenly Father as I did then. But since their death, I've faced a far deeper struggle in my immediate family, which led to much greater anxiety and fear, especially when all signs pointed to losing my marriage and family. This was the most powerful spiritual experience of my life because I clearly saw and accepted that, if my God didn't intervene, my family was doomed. I experienced intense depression and reached the limits of my endurance and ability. I realized I couldn't change my circumstances, and I was alone among humanity, yet not alone from my great, loving, heavenly Father. I was overwhelmed by the feeling (a lie) that no one wanted to be around me. I was alone with people. But God! His presence became more and more real to me. This reality was more than a feeling. There was a deep, internal awareness of His abiding presence that assured me that no matter the outcome, He was with me and was my security and hope. He was all I had, but He was all I needed.

I Desire You More than Anything or Anyone on Earth

When you focus on yourself during these difficult times, painful loneliness often results; however, if you acknowledge that Jesus is with you (Proverbs 3:6; Hebrews 13:5b), your loneliness can transform into a painless, peaceful, and secure solitude (Isaiah 43:2–3). Hebrews 2:18 (NLT) states, "Since he himself has gone through suffering and testing, he is able to help us when we are being tested." As the sinless God-Man, Jesus learned obedience through suffering; we who have sin sloshing around within us must learn obedience through our suffering. As you may know, Jesus' suffering included being abandoned on the cross by His Father for our eternal salvation. So, isn't it reasonable for you to be willing to experience loneliness from people, even those once close to you, to gain a deeper closeness with Jesus and bring Him glory? In his helpful book *Walking with God Through Pain and Suffering*, Timothy Keller writes, "As a man who seemed about to lose both his career and his family once said to me, 'I always knew, in principle, that Jesus is all you need to get through. But you don't really know Jesus is all you need until Jesus is all you have.'"[vii]

If you choose to live in the freedom of the truth that Jesus is all you have of eternal importance and priority, it will demonstrate that His presence is sufficient and of the utmost importance, even when rejected by all. When you choose to live this way, you prove your trust in the truth revealed in Isaiah 43:2–3a: "When you pass through the waters, I will be with you; and through the rivers, they will not overflow you. When you walk through the fire, you will not be scorched, nor will the flame burn you. For I am Yahweh your God, the Holy One of Israel, your Savior."

To learn the lessons our Father has for us when experiencing loneliness, we need to be willing to accept not only the lessons but also the strategy He uses to teach them. Some loneliness may result from sinful choices, but this is not always the case (e.g., David's hiding from Saul in the cave of Adullam). Regardless of the cause, it's vital to ask the Lord to reveal what He wants you to learn from this season or lifelong journey. Ask Him, "Is it related to my character, family, ministry, or something else, Lord? Please, Father, teach me. I'm willing. I know You don't condemn me (Romans 8:1), and I am eternally grateful for Your mercy. Therefore, I ask that You pour out Your lavish grace on me by granting me a deep, abiding relationship with You, so I may be still and know that You are my God" (Psalm 46:10), and that you are my God who is enough.

Through my family's trials, I learned to trust and find deeper rest in Jesus, realizing I desired Him more than anything or anyone on earth (Psalm 73:25). Although it was the most painful and loneliest time of my life, it was also the most intimate season I have experienced with Jesus. I recognized that I was experiencing a broken and contrite heart (Psalm 51:17). This reverent process fostered deep humility about my sin, genuine remorse, and the freedom to fully admit my sinfulness. I no longer felt the need to defend myself, justify my behavior, or explain my choices. There was no need to make excuses, clarify my actions, or blame others for my circumstances. This was very freeing. Even though I didn't understand everything that was happening, choosing to shift my focus away from myself and saying yes to whatever God had for me brought deep peace and a realization that I was not lonely, as I experienced a profound sense of intimacy and communion.

Nevertheless, this act of self-denial unexpectedly opened the way to embrace God's testing and discipline with a sincere desire to learn the lessons He had in store. No matter what God's reasons are for your loneliness, it is unwise not to seek what He wants to teach you through them (Romans 5:3–5; James 1:12). In circumstances like this, you have the opportunity to imitate the apostle Paul, who was willing to endure the suffering of Christ and even to lose all things to know Jesus deeply (Philippians 3:7–10).

Whether it's loneliness or any other kind of suffering or trial, God's purpose is to guide you toward self-surrender and complete reliance on Christ. Choosing self-denial doesn't mean you'll never feel loneliness again, but if you do, you can offer it to God as a sacrifice of gratitude and praise. Elisabeth Elliot said, "Loneliness itself is material for sacrifice. God has offered you something, and you have said, 'Yes, Lord, I will take it.' And accepting it and offering it back to Him with thanksgiving is then in itself material for sacrifice. I have found this to be a life-changing fact."[viii]

Although my circumstances were extremely painful and I felt isolated from others, I realized I wasn't alone, and I wouldn't trade the depth of my communion with Christ for anything or anyone. I wonder if this is what Job was contemplating when he said, "Though He slay me, I will hope in Him" (13:15).

In Acceptance Lies Peace

Are you willing to accept God's will no matter what happens? In the following, Elliot makes some critical distinctions of motives related to God's will:

> God is looking for men and women to say, "Yes, Lord," no matter what happens. By "yes," I mean a voluntary, willed choice. I don't mean a resignation or a weary or some sort of lazy acceptance: "Oh, what else can I do? I don't have any other choice"; a helpless acquiescence; or a teeth-gritting, white-knuckle, fist-clenching, "Well, if this is what you are going to do to me, I guess I'll have to take it because I really don't have a choice."[ix]

Elliot answered this question for herself: "I can testify with all my heart that in acceptance lieth peace. And by 'acceptance,' I mean a simple willed act of saying, 'Lord, I don't like it, I don't understand it, I don't know how I am going to bear it, but by Your grace I will take it. My answer is yes.'"[x]

The apostle Peter records not only God's protection during loneliness (or any trial), but also its benefits:

> And through your faith, God is protecting you by his power until you receive this salvation, which is ready to be revealed on the last day for all to see. So be truly glad. There is wonderful joy ahead, even though you must endure many trials for a little while. These trials will show that your faith is genuine. It is being tested as fire tests and purifies gold—though your faith is far more precious than mere gold. So when your

faith remains strong through many trials, it will bring you much praise
and glory and honor on the day when Jesus Christ is revealed to the
whole world.

1 Peter 1:5–7, NLT

Although what we experience is only a small part of our Savior's
suffering, rejection, and loneliness, He wants us to acknowledge our
feelings of isolation while also remembering that He endured separation
from His Father—something we are assured will never happen to us. We
are guaranteed that even in our darkest, most painful moments, we will
never be abandoned by God (Hebrews 13:5), even if those closest to us
have turned away. Additionally, we are also reminded that no one, nothing, can truly separate us from God's love, not even our own sin!
(Romans 8:37–39) That's why God reminds you that, even if accusations, true or false, are made against you, since you belong to Him, He
calls you a conqueror, even when those near you see you as a failure and
avoid you. They are not your judge, and neither are you. God is your
Judge, and He has declared you not guilty.

A Lonely Bird That Is Not Alone

Have you ever felt like a lonely, solitary bird sitting on a rooftop,
watching all the activity while realizing that, not only does no one see
you, but no one cares about you? In his commentary on Psalm 102,
Warren W. Wiersbe makes the following helpful comments:

God enjoys endless years, but we endure shortened days (vv. 23–24),
troubled days (v. 2), days that disappear like smoke, grass, and a shadow
(vv. 3, 4, 11). We sit alone like birds in a desert and dying patients in a
hospital (vv. 5–9). How depressing! Do you ever have days like that? If
you do, beware. Looking at yourself and your feelings will only make
things worse. Do what the writer of this penitential psalm did: look by
faith to the Lord. Things will be different when you look from yourself
to God and say, "But You."

"But You shall endure" (vv. 12–22). If you know Jesus Christ by
faith, you possess eternal life (1 John 5:11–13). So, living in a world of
death and decay need not be a threat to you because you will live
forever with the Lord (1 Thessalonians 4:13–18).

"But You are the same" (vv. 25–28). As you grow older, you may find yourself resisting change. Loved ones move away or die, your body weakens, the world changes, and it is easy to become bitter and afraid. But God does not change (Heb. 13:5–8), and He is your Friend and Guide to the very end (Psalm 73:24).

The temporary things will change, but the things eternal will last (2 Corinthians 4:11–18).[xi]

We are reminded that as Christians, we are to have a distinct perspective and response to the losses, trials, and sorrows in our lives. This truth is seen in 1 Thessalonians 4:13, "But we do not want you to be uninformed, brothers, about those who are asleep, so that you will not grieve as do the rest who have no hope." Christians have a distinct hope in the One who died for us on the cross. Sometimes our hopes are realized on this side of death, and sometimes they are not. As a young boy, I would often play under the quilt my mom and aunts were working on above me. When I looked at the bottom of the quilt, it was tattered, distorted, and in no way attractive. However, when I moved out from under the quilt and viewed the other side, I saw the beauty, color, detail, and magnificent design of what the women were creating. In principle, the same is true of the heavenly quilt our Father is creating in our individual lives. By His design, while on earth, we only view the unfinished portion. But one day, we will come to the other side and experience a place beyond our imagination, as recorded in 1 Corinthians 2:9: "But just as it is written, 'Things which eye has not seen and ear has not heard, and which have not entered the heart of man, all that God has prepared for those who love Him'" (Also see Isaiah 64:4, 65:17).

Regardless of our feelings, we hold to the truth that our God is sovereign over all of our lives and circumstances, and He is good and loves us. Therefore, we trust Him that the life He is weaving through the hardships, pain, and sin in our lives will result in a masterful and eternal life to His glory. Even though we can't see the other side, here are two verses that instruct us how to live while on earth:

So we don't look at the troubles we can see now; rather, we fix our gaze on things that cannot be seen. For the things we see now will soon be gone, but the things we cannot see will last forever.

2 CORINTHIANS 4:18 NLT

> For I consider that the sufferings of this present time are not worthy to
> be compared with the glory that is to be revealed to us.
>   ROMANS 8:18

Of Psalm 142, Derek Kidner rightly says, "In [it] the strain of being hated and hunted is almost too much, and faith is at full stretch." Yes, but David is not defeated, and in the final words, his faith "is at last joined by hope."[xii]

J. M. Boice adds this personal experience:

> What does it take to lift our prayers from the wasteland of mere routine to the high ground of actually pleading with Jehovah? One thing that seems to work well is trouble, the very thing we are considering in this study. In easy times our prayers are easy too, but they take on a new urgency when trouble comes. The same day I sat down to write this chapter, I received a letter from South Africa telling me that one of my friends, a leader in the church in Johannesburg, had collapsed at work and was diagnosed with a brain tumor. He had an operation, received a guarded prognosis, and at the moment I received the letter seemed to be doing fine. It had been a frightening occurrence. His testimony is that this was the most important spiritual experience of his life, since it threw him on God in new ways. When there are none to help but God, Christians do learn to trust him, and they find that he is attentive to their cries.[xiii]

I find it somewhat easier to handle when casual acquaintances decide they no longer want to be around me. However, when relatives, neighbors, coworkers, and especially immediate family members—many of whom I see regularly, some daily—turn away, it feels like having an organ removed without anesthesia. If you can relate to this, you can also understand our brother Job, for he tells us, "He (God) has removed my brothers far from me, and my acquaintances are completely estranged from me. My relatives have failed, and my familiar friends have forgotten me" (Job 19:13–14).

All of this leads to feeling like that lonely bird in Psalm 102:7. But remember the unusual paradox, "aloneness is presence." It's true that loneliness is a deep, painful experience and a common one. But I promise you, if you turn to Jesus even in your darkest moments (Psalm 23:4) and cry out to Him to be your closest companion (no human relationship can match this) and are patient, He will answer your desperate prayer by revealing Himself in unexpected but deeply personal ways. Throughout Scripture, intimacy with Yahweh is experienced through trust and waiting (Proverbs 3:5–6; Isaiah 40:31). These qualities may not be popular in the world today, but they were common among the godly men and women in Scripture and remain among His holy ones today. Choosing to live in the truth of trusting and waiting not only deepens your relationship with Jesus but also helps you see your circumstances as under your Lord's sovereign care and control. While you wait, commit to actively participating in your local church's worship service and to reaching out to serve your brothers and sisters (Hebrews 10:24–25), knowing that Jesus is with you and desires for you to experience Him through the people you will spend eternity with in heaven. Isolation is not your friend. It's quite common for Jesus to fill the lonely void in our lives when we surround ourselves with members of our eternal family.

I suggest listening to the following songs: "No Longer Lonely" by Robert Harkness (1920), "I Am Not Alone" by Kari Jobe (2014), and "Not Alone" by Eddie B (2016).

Small-group Discussion Questions

1. What is your biggest fear about being alone? Explain.

2. Explain how it's possible to feel lonely despite being in a crowd.

3. If you were sitting on a park bench and suddenly realized Jesus was sitting beside you, would you feel lonely? How would you relate your answer to what Paul says in Galatians 2:20 about Christ's residence?

Suggestions for Freedom from Loneliness

1. What application can you make to your present loneliness in light of Hebrews 13:5b: "I will never desert you, nor will I ever forsake you?"

2. Whom could you invite over for dinner, grab coffee with, do a Zoom meeting with, or call on the phone? When you're with them, ask them to pray for you that the Lord would fill your void.

3. Pray for the Lord to direct you to a place where you can assist those in need.

Chapter Ten

FREEDOM TO WORSHIP GOD IN SPIRIT AND TRUTH

*But an hour is coming, and now is, when the true worshipers
will worship the Father in spirit and truth; for such people
the Father seeks to be His worshipers. God is spirit, and those
who worship Him must worship in spirit and truth.*
JOHN 4:23–24

Baseball or Worship?

My life goal in high school was to become a professional baseball player.
During my senior year, I was invited to a three-day professional tryout.
This was my chance to start pursuing that goal. The night before the
tryout, I went to the church building I attended and tried to make a deal
with God. I said something like, "If you allow me to get signed by the
pros, I will do whatever you want." My request was simple, straightfor-
ward, and completely God-centered . . . I mean, self-centered. I wasn't
thinking about God and His deserved glory; I wanted my will and
hoped God would grant it. In other words, my greatest inclination
(remember chapter two regarding your will?) was pride and worldly
passions. That meant I always chose from the table of sin, which also
included my attempt to get a signed contract from God. I had no desire
to select from the table of righteousness; it wasn't an option. Even
though my behavior might have appeared to the casual observer like a

religious person asking God for a contract, I was like a Pharisee—inside I was a whitewashed tomb full of dead men's bones (Matthew 23:27). There was no consideration for God, His glory, nor any desire or ability to worship Him. But three years later, when my eyes were opened, and I became a follower of Jesus, the Spirit of God started illuminating my mind with His Word. I had received God's truth, and through the Holy Spirit's work of sanctification, I began to see how I could experience God's freedom whenever I was overwhelmed with any of the negative feelings mentioned throughout this book, as well as any form of inner bondage that the world, flesh, and devil offered me.

Later in my Christian life, I read John 4:23–24 and was surprised to learn that God has standards for worshiping Him. In the context of these two verses, Jesus introduces an immoral Samaritan woman to true worship—the kind that pleases our heavenly Father. I wanted to worship God, but I didn't really understand what worship was or how to worship in spirit and truth.

True worship honors the nature and attributes of Yahweh, as well as what He has done, is doing, and will do. Both are to be expressed with a reverent and awe-filled attitude of gratitude. We see an example of this in Hebrews 12:28–29: "Therefore, since we are receiving a kingdom which cannot be shaken, let us show gratitude, by which we may offer to God an acceptable service with reverence and awe; for our God is a consuming fire."

For many years, I believed the Sunday morning worship service was about fellowship with Christians, listening to God's Word, and singing hymns. But one day, I wondered whether worship and singing hymns were the same thing. Do you need to be inside a church building to worship? Is music and singing necessary to worship God? The answers are found in Romans 12:1 NKJV: "I beseech you therefore, brethren, by the mercies of God, that you present your bodies a living sacrifice, holy, acceptable to God, which is your reasonable service." This verse contains much truth about worship, and in this final chapter, I will answer six questions about worshiping Yahweh.

1. What Is Needed for Acceptable Worship?

Acceptable worship is more than just a ritual or ceremony performed on Sunday mornings. Instead, the ability to worship God acceptably depends on your spirit, heart, and mind being guided by the Holy Spirit through the truth of Scripture. The prophet Ezekiel, when writing about the future new covenant, reveals what every believer receives when genuine faith is expressed:

> Moreover, I will give you a new heart and put a new spirit within you; and I will remove the heart of stone from your flesh and give you a heart of flesh. I will put My Spirit within you and cause you to walk in My statutes, and you will be careful to do My judgments.
> EZEKIEL 36:26–27

In these two verses, four essential aspects relate to your salvation and worship of God. First, you received a new heart. Why was a new heart necessary? According to Jeremiah 17:9, all hearts of nonbelievers are deceitful and desperately sick. These hearts are marked by deceit and cannot be trusted. Additionally, Jeremiah depicts these hearts as spiritually weak, defined by wickedness and an incurable state known only to God (Jeremiah 15:18). Second, you received a new spirit. You needed a new spirit because you were spiritually dead in your sins and were unable to have a relationship with God, do good, or obey God (Romans 3:10–12; Ephesians 2:1). Third, you received the Holy Spirit, who is God's seal and guarantee of your salvation (Ephesians 1:13–14). Also, according to Jeremiah 31:33, God says, "I will put My law within them, and on their heart I will write it; and I will be their God, and they shall be My people." Fourth, the Holy Spirit will cause you to walk in God's statutes (Ezekiel 36:27). Notice the word *cause*, which indicates the work of the Holy Spirit in your heart. This echoes Augustine's prayer, "Oh God, grant what thou dost command and command what thou dost desire." You see that without the Holy Spirit's help, you are unable to understand or obey God's commands, nor can you give Yahweh the proper worship He deserves.

A recurring theme in the psalms is the call for God's people to worship their great God and King. In Psalm 29, David uses a compelling approach to encourage his audience to deepen their worship of Yahweh by highlighting examples of the heavenly angels. The entire psalm centers on the angels' praise and worship of Yahweh. Throughout these eleven verses, David mentions God's personal name, Yahweh (I Am), eighteen times, emphasizing that He is the angels' focus of worship. David states that Yahweh's holy name deserves the angels' glory and praise. He describes a thunderstorm, saying that Yahweh thunders over the waters (vv. 3–9). It's possible that David wrote this psalm during a thunderstorm. My wife loves thunderstorms because they remind her of God's mighty power. Even though Yahweh's mighty power shakes the earth during the storm, my wife feels His peace. This idea is reflected in vv. 10–11, "Yahweh sat enthroned over the flood; indeed, Yahweh sits as King forever. Yahweh will give strength to His people; Yahweh will bless His people with peace." Wouldn't this psalm make a great devotional reading for children during a fierce storm or a meaningful worship experience during a thunderstorm while the pastor teaches? Both activities could conclude with what David proclaims at the end of verse 9: "And in His temple everything says, 'Glory!'" So, we see David's psalm begins in heaven with the praise of angels to Yahweh and moves to earth, ending with the people of God proclaiming, "Glory to Yahweh!"

As you can see, the main focus of Psalm 29 is on praising and worshiping Yahweh. Essentially, this is your purpose on earth—to glorify God by offering yourself as a living and holy sacrifice, which is your "reasonable" service of worship. Praise God for the blessings of the new covenant recorded in Ezekiel 36:26–27—a new heart, a new spirit, and the Holy Spirit who empowers obedience—because you are now free to fully worship Yahweh like the angels described in Psalm 29:1–11. Your worship can now be experienced with reverence and pure devotion as you glorify Yahweh alone.

2. How Does God Want You to Worship Him?

Now that we have identified some of the blessings God has given you through the new covenant for eternal life and acceptable worship, let's explore the meaning of the two criteria necessary for acceptable worship. You must worship in spirit and truth. This is very different from the worship of the Old Testament Jews and the Samaritan woman Jesus spoke to.

The Samaritans' worship was marked by intense emotion and

enthusiasm; however, their passion was not rooted in truth. They believed only in the first five books of the Old Testament (the Law, or Pentateuch), missing the insights from the remaining thirty-four books, which revealed more about who Yahweh was and how He should be worshiped. In contrast, the Jews, who accepted the entire Old Testament, had a much deeper understanding of doctrinal truth. Yet, for many, this resulted in a form of intellectual worship characterized by cold, external ceremonies and a lack of genuine heartfelt devotion to Yahweh (Isaiah 29:13; Matthew 15:8). In summary, both the Samaritans and the Jews worshiped but lacked either truth or devotion.

Many churches today have chosen either the emotional approach of the Samaritans or the intellectual approach of the Jews. The Samaritan style of worship has led to highly emotional and thoughtless activities that have caused many people to go astray. Meanwhile, the intellectual method results in cold legalism and sterile congregations. Neither of these approaches is acceptable for true worship of Yahweh.

"In spirit" does not refer to the Holy Spirit but to the new human spirit you received, which replaced your dead spirit. Receiving this new spirit from God enables you to surrender yourself entirely to Him, abide intimately, and worship Him acceptably. The kind of worship God requires is "internal" worship made possible by the Holy Spirit (Philippians 3:3), through your new spirit, not based on external ceremonies or rituals, but from your new heart.

Worship in truth means your inner worship must align appropriately with the truth of God's Word, focusing on the triune God. There is a lesson to be learned from Aaron's two sons, Nadab and Abihu, who were priests and offered strange fire on the altar of incense. Fire came out from Yahweh's presence and consumed them, causing their deaths before Yahweh. After this sinful act, Moses spoke with Aaron, his brother and high priest, reiterating what Yahweh said: "By those who come near Me I will be treated as holy, and before all the people I will be glorified. So Aaron kept silent" (Leviticus 10:3b; Exodus 30:8). According to 1 Peter 2:9, every Christian is a possession of God and a member of His royal priesthood. Therefore, it is wise to remember what Moses told Aaron. About 700 years later, we learn about the highest expression of Yahweh's holiness from Isaiah's vision:

> In the year of King Uzziah's death I saw the Lord sitting on a throne, high and lifted up, with the train of His robe filling the temple.

Seraphim stood above Him, each having six wings: with two he covered his face, and with two he covered his feet, and with two he flew. And one called out to another and said, "Holy, Holy, Holy, is Yahweh of hosts; the whole earth is full of His glory." And the foundations of the thresholds shook at the voice of him who called out, while the house of God was filling with smoke.

Isaiah 6:1–4

Yahweh has not changed; He is holy and must always be honored as such, especially by His family of priests, who are to present their entire being daily as a living and holy sacrifice. This requires confession throughout the day as we worship Yahweh in spirit and truth.

Acceptable worship does not require music, even when it is filled with solid doctrine; nor is doctrinally sound music unacceptable for worship. Although music isn't essential for worship, I find that when it accompanies the solid doctrines of the faith, my heart is lifted in praise, leading to spiritual communion and worship of the triune God.

The apostle John clearly states that the two essential elements for acceptable worship that your heavenly Father seeks in His children are "in spirit and truth." Therefore, we are to avoid mindless passion and cold intellectualism, but worship God from a pure and devoted heart led by the truth of Scripture.

3. How Do You Present Your Body as a Living and Holy Sacrifice?

Because of Adam's willful sin, we see God's justice, mercy, and grace in providing animal skins for Adam and Eve. These skins came from the first sacrifice for sin, seen in Genesis 3:21. This marked the beginning of a fifteen-century period (from 1440 BC to AD 70) during which Yahweh taught Israel about His holiness, justice, faithfulness, mercy, and grace. All of this was accomplished through establishing a sacrificial system centered around the tabernacle, which housed the ark of the covenant—the very presence of holy Yahweh among His unholy people. The old covenant sacrificial system involved five main sacrifices offered at the bronze altar in the tabernacle courtyard. First were burnt offerings, which signified devotion, commitment, thanksgiving, or atonement for sin (Exodus 29:38–42; Psalm 51:16–17; Leviticus 1). Second were grain offerings, which served as a gift to the Sovereign Lord and acknowledgment of their covenant relationship (Numbers 28:1–8; Leviticus 2:1–2, 13). Third were peace (fellowship) offerings, a sacrificial meal shared between the offeror and Yahweh to strengthen their bond (Numbers 6:14; Leviticus 3:1–17, 7:11–21). Fourth were sin offerings, involving different animals for sins committed against God (Leviticus 4:5–13, 6:24–30; Numbers 15:1–12). Fifth were guilt offerings, which addressed sins against other people (Leviticus 4:5–13, 6:24–30, 7:11; Numbers 15:1–12; Hebrews 8:3, 9:11–14, 10:1–4, 18–22).

These five dead sacrifices foreshadowed Christ's ultimate sacrifice on the cross. His sacrificial death fulfilled the old covenant by providing a permanent satisfaction of God's wrath against us (propitiation, 1 John 2:2) and a permanent removal of our sins (expiation, Psalm 103:12). But unlike all the old covenant sacrifices that were once killed and remained dead, Jesus, being sinless and unjustly killed, defeated death by rising from the dead to live forever. Therefore, sacrifices are no longer needed or required. Instead, we are told what God desires in Hosea 6:6 (NASB): "For I delight in loyalty rather than sacrifice, and in the knowledge of God rather than burnt offerings." Here, Hosea combines spirit and truth, revealing what Yahweh delights in from His followers.

During Hosea's ministry, the Jews relied on outward ceremonies and rituals, losing sight of genuine love for Yahweh. Today, this superficial form of worship remains common. Many are content with the service's liturgy, and they focus on the pastor's or priest's attire, the church building, the cathedral's grandeur, or the beauty of the stained-glass windows. Those who focus on these external things are often satisfied with the mere rules, rituals, and routines of external worship. While others come to a stage performance featuring blaring music, smoke, and flashing lights, all with the intent of being entertained; they fail to recognize that these things are despised by God (1 Samuel 15:22; Isaiah 1:11–20; Micah 6:6–8), for He seeks broken and contrite hearts (Psalm 51:17; Isaiah 66:2; Matthew 5:3; Luke 18:9–14). They give little attention to the fact that the creator God desires their love and loyalty, expressed through intimacy, heartfelt obedience, and service rooted in true gratitude (Hosea 6:6; Hebrews 12:28–29).

Yahweh emphasizes that His desire is for inner devotion and loyalty, which will always show outwardly, but the opposite is not true. Simply attending church, giving money, or offering lip service from a cold heart will not fool Him. He clearly states that superficial ceremonies and rituals are always rejected when a loving relationship is absent (Isaiah 29:13; Ezekiel 33:31; Matthew 15:7–9).

The truths of Hosea 6:6 were important to Jesus, as he quoted from them twice (Matthew 9:13, 12:7) to expose the hypocrisy of the religious leaders. The Son of God wanted the same thing as His Father—love and closeness with God. D. A. Garrett insightfully states,

> This does not mean that Hosea regarded sacrifice or ritual worship as intrinsically bad, and it should not prompt us to suppose that the path to spirituality is to overthrow all liturgy and formal worship. In modern language one might appropriately rephrase this verse as, "I desire devotion and not hymn-singing, service and not sermons," without thereby concluding that hymns and sermons were evil.[i]

Commentator C. Simeon offers a clear and practical observation in the following:

> There is a disposition in every man to substitute external observances for the devotion of the heart; and to rest satisfied with rendering to God some easy services, while they are utterly averse to those duties which are more difficult and self-denying. But God cannot be deceived, nor will he be mocked. He will look at the heart, and not at the outward appearance only; and will mark with indignation the partial obedience of the hypocrite, no less than the open disobedience of the profane. It was thus that he dealt with his people of old, "hewing them by his prophets, and slaying them by the words of his mouth," because they rested in their sacrifices and burnt-offerings, when he desired the more acceptable services of faith and love.[ii]

Therefore, since Jesus died for your sins once for all time, you are called to live a life of sacrifice for Him forever in love, loyalty, and worship. Since Jesus' crucifixion, all acceptable sacrifices to God are to be living sacrifices. This truth is reflected in Romans 12:1 NKJV: "I beseech you therefore, brethren, by the mercies of God, that you present your bodies a living sacrifice, holy, acceptable to God, which is your reasonable service."

4. What Is the Purpose of Your Spiritual Service of Worship?

In John 4:23, Jesus refers to God as "Father," teaching that Yahweh is His Father and the Father of every follower of Jesus. Jesus uses this term *father* (*patér*) sixty-five times in the Synoptic Gospels (Matthew, Mark, and Luke), including seventeen times in the Sermon on the Mount (Matthew 5–7). John, the beloved disciple, uses the word father more than a hundred times in his gospel. Additionally, Jesus uses a particularly endearing term when He addresses His Father as "Abba" (Mark 14:36). "Jesus probably used *abbá* for God not only in Mark 14:36 but also whenever the Greek patér occurs. It denotes childlike intimacy and trust, not disrespect. It undoubtedly expresses the new relationship with God proclaimed and lived out by Jesus and then experienced by believers in him."[iii]

As the apostle Paul emphasizes, every believer inherits all the spiritual blessings in the heavenly places in Christ (Ephesians 1:3). We learn that these blessings include permanent adoption into God's eternal, spiritual family (Ephesians 1:5). This family kingdom is an intimate community where each of God's children (John 1:12), following Jesus' example, can address God as "Abba Father" (Romans 8:15; Galatians 4:6). Therefore, because of the Father-child relationship graciously given to us, we can respond to our Abba's love with heartfelt worship. Since God is spirit, our worship must be genuine, in spirit and truth, empowered by the Holy Spirit, who is the Spirit of Truth (John 14:17), guiding us into deep, heartfelt intimacy regardless of our location or circumstances. In summary, the purpose of our spiritual worship is holistic communion with God, encompassing all of our heart, soul, mind, and strength (Mark 12:30).

But what does it mean to commune with Yahweh with all your heart, soul, mind, and strength? The Shema is a Jewish prayer that expresses Judaism's core beliefs and emphasizes monotheism. This prayer was usually recited every morning and evening, serving as both an individual and national declaration worth risking one's life for. It is as follows:

Hear, O Israel! Yahweh is our God, Yahweh is one! You shall love Yahweh your God with all your heart and with all your soul and with all your might. These words, which I am commanding you today, shall be on your heart. You shall teach them diligently to your sons and shall speak of them when you sit in your house and when you walk by the way and when you lie down and when you rise up. You shall bind them as a sign on your hand, and they shall be as phylacteries between your eyes. You shall write them on the doorposts of your house and on your gates.

Deuteronomy 6:4–9

The Shema in the Old Testament includes what Jesus called the Great Commandment. This commandment lists three human faculties —heart, soul, and might—for loving Yahweh, but in the Synoptic Gospels, Jesus added a fourth—your mind. In the original Greek, these four faculties are interconnected and overlap to some extent. The following is a list of these faculties:

- **Heart**: volitional and emotional capacities, including your thoughts.
- **Soul**: your life and personality as a whole, separate from your body.
- **Mind**: understanding, intellect, beliefs, attitudes, values, and will.
- **Might**: physical and mental strength, including moral power.

Obeying the Greatest Commandment doesn't mean dividing your life into four parts to love Yahweh. Instead, the Jewish intention is to love and worship Yahweh wholeheartedly, with all of your being and existence, without leaving anything out or holding anything back.

5. Where Is Worship Acceptable?

Not only did God want to be worshiped, but He also longed to dwell among His people forever. We see the beginning of this in God's command to Moses in Exodus 25:8–9: "And let them make a sanctuary for Me, that I may dwell among them. According to all that I am going to show you, as the pattern of the tabernacle and the pattern of all its furniture, just so you shall make it." This tabernacle was the first of eight temples recorded in the Bible.

1. The Tabernacle (Exodus 25–30, 40:38; Leviticus 10:1–7)

2. Solomon's temple (2 Samuel 7:1–29; 1 Kings 8:1–66; Jeremiah 32:28–44)

3. Zerubbabel's temple (Ezra 3:1–8, 4:1–14, 6:1–22)

4. Herod's temple (Mark 13:2, 14–23; Luke 1:11–20, 2:22–38, 42–51, 4:21–24; Acts 21:27–33)

5. The heart of every believer (1 Corinthians 3:16, 6:19–20; 2 Corinthians 6:16–18)

6. Tribulation temple (Daniel 9:24–27, 12:11; Matthew 24:15; 2 Thessalonians 2:4; Revelation 11:1–2, 13:14–15)

7. Millennial temple (Isaiah 2:2–3; Ezekiel 40–42; Zechariah 6:12–13)

8. Eternal temple—the Father and the Son (Revelation 21:22, 22:1–21)

Biblical temples were built for corporate worship of Yahweh, but He has always desired worship from a pure, sincere heart. Now, every new covenant believer is empowered by the Holy Spirit to worship with a new heart and spirit.

Both the Jews and the Samaritans focused their worship on physical objects. Because the Samaritans accepted only the Pentateuch as authoritative, they chose Mount Gerizim for their worship (Genesis 12:6–7; Deuteronomy 11:29). In contrast, the Jews accepted the entire Old Testament as authoritative and believed Yahweh chose the Jerusalem temple as the place of corporate worship (2 Chronicles 6:6; Psalm 48:1–2). Jesus' response to the Samaritan woman likely surprised both her and the Jews by indicating that a time was coming when acceptable worship would no longer be confined to either Mount Gerizim or Jerusalem. When the Jerusalem temple was destroyed a few decades after Jesus' declaration to the Samaritan woman, the new covenant had already been established, making all external ceremonies and rituals unnecessary. The old covenant law was fulfilled and replaced by the new covenant, established through Jesus' blood. Therefore, true worshipers are those who worship the Father in spirit and truth, regardless of location. Over time, the place of worship shifted from the mobile tabernacle to the permanent Jerusalem temple and then to the hearts of every believer (1 Corinthians 3:16, 6:19–20; 2 Corinthians 6:16–18).

6. What Is a Reasonable Motivator for Worshiping Yahweh?

The challenge of winning your daily spiritual battles can sometimes feel confusing and overwhelming. However, Scripture states that victory comes from asking the Holy Spirit for His help (Galatians 5:16) and choosing to walk in the truth (2 John 1:4b), regardless of how you feel.

Romans 12:1 (NKJV) reads, "I beseech you therefore, brethren, by the mercies of God, that you present your bodies a living sacrifice, holy, acceptable to God, which is your reasonable service." Paul uses six key words that I want to explain and demonstrate how he integrates these terms to show how your worship can be pleasing to God.

1. **Beseech**: Paul is calling these believers and urging them to adopt a specific way of life.

2. **Mercies**: Paul's motivating truth is God's mercies. Mercy can be understood as all that God withholds from us that we rightfully deserve because of our sin. According to Romans 6:23, the payment for sin is eternal death. In other words, every individual sin we commit deserves God's just judgment of the eternal lake of fire. But because of God's abundant mercies extended to us through faith in Christ, He withholds this judgment from us every day since Jesus has already paid for it (propitiation). Since God is "the Father of mercies and the God of all comfort" (2 Corinthians 1:3), it is not surprising that His mercies are available to us every morning (Lamentations 3:22–23) for any sin we commit that day. Therefore, out of gratitude, the apostle Paul calls us to present our bodies as a living sacrifice.

3. **Body**: Paul's use of the word *body* does not only refer to our physical bodies. He uses this term to encompass a holistic view of our entire being. In other words, consider the holistic elements of the Great Commandment seen in our heart, soul, mind, and strength. Paul wants you to offer your entire being—everything that makes you, you—as a holy sacrifice to Yahweh, for this pleases Him.

4. **Living**: All animal sacrifices related to the Old Covenant had to die. But because Jesus died and conquered death by rising from the tomb, God no longer requires dead sacrifices.

5. **Holy**: We are not only called to present ourselves as a living sacrifice but also as a holy sacrifice. "Holy" implies being set apart for God and maintaining moral purity, because God is holy (1 Peter 1:16).

6. **Reasonable**: This term relates to our rational abilities. As a Christian, the standard and safeguard for our reasoning is God's Word (Psalm 119:9, 11). To grow in practical holiness and righteousness, our reasoning should never be based on our feelings or on what man says, because, according to Jesus, our sanctification comes through the Word of God (John 17:17). Our reasoning must always be grounded in biblical truth.

In summary, Paul is encouraging Christians, based on all the mercies God has given, is giving, and will continue to give, to present our entire being as both a living and holy sacrifice daily. This is not only a reasonable way to live but also a path to freedom. Therefore, no matter where we are, how we feel, or what our circumstances are, we can choose to follow Paul's instruction in 1 Corinthians 10:31: "Whether, then, you eat or drink or whatever you do, do all to the glory of God."

A Reminder About Choices

As we reflect on God's daily mercies that He continually pours out on us (Lamentations 3:22–23; Romans 12:1a; Titus 3:5), we are led to love and worship God and to love others. Before I move on, I want to highlight an encouraging truth recorded in Psalm 8:4: "What is man that You remember him, and the son of man that You care for him?" Oh, Abba Father, thank you for remembering and caring for me.

A practical definition of the agape love that God has for you and desires for you to have for Him and others is found in 1 Corinthians 13:4–7 (NLT). Take a moment to read these verses and notice that the manifestation of agape love is not based on feelings; rather, it is a choice to do what is right, grounded in truth.

> Love is patient and kind. Love is not jealous or boastful or proud or rude. It does not demand its own way. It is not irritable, and it keeps no record of being wronged. It does not rejoice about injustice but rejoices whenever the truth wins out. Love never gives up, never loses faith, is always hopeful, and endures through every circumstance.

Although you were freed from slavery to sin when you became a new creation in Christ (2 Corinthians 5:17; Galatians 2:20), sin still resides in your physical, mortal body, which is the part that dies and turns to dust (Romans 6 and 7). This temporary vessel, including your mind, remains the ongoing battleground where the spiritual fight occurs. You know this struggle is real because the sin within you battles against your sanctification every day.

To overcome negative feelings, urges, and temptations (the table of sin), you can abide in Christ daily (John 15:5) by immersing yourself in God's Word and prayer, thereby returning love to God and demonstrating obedience (John 14:21). These daily practices will help you walk by the Spirit (Galatians 5:16) and cultivate inclinations that guide your will toward the table of righteousness. This is how you worship each day by presenting your body as a living, holy sacrifice, ready to do your Master's work.

I highly suggest reverently listening to the hymn "Holy, Holy, Holy" by Reginald Heber (1826).

Small-group Discussion Questions

1. What does it mean to worship in spirit and truth?

2. What is the significance of worshiping God with all your heart, soul, mind, and strength?

3. What is the connection between intimacy with God and worshiping Him?

Suggestions for Freedom to Worship

1. What benefits would you gain in your life by worshiping God all day?

2. How would your life change if you recognized how merciful God is to you each day?

3. Explain why offering your entire self as a living and holy sacrifice to God in worship is considered reasonable.

SUMMARY OF PART II: BIBLICAL LIVING FOR OUR FREEDOM

(What You Can Do with God)

1. **Guilt**: The royal Judge of the universe has already declared you not guilty.

2. **Anxiety**: Don't forget the comma in 1 Peter 5:5–6. Surrender your worries and concerns to the Lord in humility, but don't take them back in pride. They now belong to Him, so choose to wait for the what, when, and how of His will.

3. **Pride**: Do you want to be like Jesus or the devil?

4. **Fear**: Reverence for Yahweh is the remedy for any sinful fear (1 John 4:18).

5. **Anger**: Choose to be slow to anger, just like your heavenly Father.

6. **Loneliness**: Desire God more than anything or anyone else on earth.

7. **Worship**: Reflect on all the mercy God has shown you for each of your sins. It is reasonable to dedicate your entire being to Him daily as a living and holy act of worship.

ENDING WITH A RACE

Therefore Pilate said to Him, "So You are a king?" Jesus answered, "You yourself said I am a king. For this I have been born, and for this I have come into the world, to bear witness to the truth. Everyone who is of the truth hears My voice." Pilate said to Him, "What is truth?"
JOHN 18:37–38a

Dennis Kinlaw wrote, "Truth should gain and control us instead of being controlled by us. There is an element of unrelenting moral demand in truth; it is other-centered. It matters not whether we have mastered truth and can use it; it matters only whether we have surrendered to truth and are willing to obey it.[i]

Your Steeplechase

The movie *Chariots of Fire* won the Best Picture Oscar in 1981. It is based on the true story of two British runners at the 1924 Olympics: Eric Liddell (played by Ian Charleson), a devout Scottish Christian who runs to glorify God, and Harold Abrahams (played by Ben Cross), an English Jew who runs for himself. Abrahams won the gold medal in the 100 meters, while Liddell took gold in the 400 meters. Liddell's famous quote from the movie is, "I believe God made me for a purpose, but He also made me fast. And when I run, I feel His pleasure." Eric serves as an example for us in our spiritual race mentioned in Hebrews 12:1–2. We don't just run *for* Jesus; we run *with* Jesus and for His pleasure.

As you know, the spiritual race you run is not a sprint but a lifelong, holy mission. While the movie focuses on Liddell and Abrahams, it also shows a brief clip of a 3,000-meter steeplechase. This tough race, run by Evelyn Montague (played by Nicholas Farrell), is not a quick sprint but an endurance test filled with obstacles that seem impossible to overcome. But remember, your spiritual steeplechase was specially designed by your Lord just for you (Hebrews 12:1). So, remembering that Jesus runs with you, keep your eyes fixed on Him with the intent to finish your race by running in truth (1 Corinthians 9:24; 2 Timothy 4:7), knowing that Jesus will use this race to strengthen your faith (Hebrews 12:2).

When I was younger, I usually ran five to six days a week, and some runs were more difficult than others. During one run, thoughts flooded my mind, and I couldn't wait to get home to write them down. This poem, filled with the truth of Scripture, has been—and still is—a source of hope and joy that encourages me to keep running in truth through my daily spiritual steeplechase.

The Responsible Christian
Up this lonely road I run, yet alone I do not go
'Tis Jesus who is with me, therefore alone I must not sow
Up this grueling mount I press, I also need to water
To give my heart and mind to Him, so run I do much harder
But the race continues, and I do reap
Yet soon 'tis Jesus who takes my soul to keep.[ii]

As you run your steeplechase, expect obstacles and ask for God's grace to persevere through them, not around them. These hurdles and stumbling blocks often include the feelings described in chapters four through nine. It would be unusual for a steeplechase runner to be surprised that his race is difficult and filled with trials. Remind yourself each morning that this day may present challenges. Peter reminds us that trials are opportunities to show that our faith is real. Your faith is genuine when you run your race in His truth, no matter the trials, circumstances, or feelings. Choosing to run this way brings praise, glory, and honor to Jesus (1 Peter 1:6–7; 1 Corinthians 1:3–7).

The key to finishing the steeplechase that Jesus uniquely designed for you isn't feelings but truth. Truth is the fuel that powers you to persevere and complete your race. Focusing on negative feelings won't help; they will only weigh you down and make each step harder and heavier. Living under the burden of feelings will slow your spiritual growth, while focusing on truth gives a burst of spiritual adrenaline to keep moving forward.

Many times, during my runs, I talked to myself. I was encouraged to learn that the psalmists also practiced self-talk, especially when facing negative feelings. Consider Psalm 42:5: "Why are you in despair, O my soul? And why are you disturbed within me? Wait for God, for I shall still praise Him, for the salvation of His presence."

The purpose of your steeplechase is to shape the character of Jesus in you because this is essential for the upward call of God in Christ Jesus (Philippians 3:14). But remember, the New Testament doesn't tell you to follow the path Jesus walked but rather to follow Jesus Himself (Luke 9:23). When you keep your eyes on Jesus (not the race), He will guide you and empower you to run the race He has set before you. Being anxious or fearful are examples of focusing on the race and not Jesus. The key truth to hold onto is that your steeplechase is personal and relational. Just like the apostle Paul, your new life has been given to you so you can know (be intimate with) Jesus (Philippians 3:7–11). Jesus' main goal on earth was to glorify His heavenly Father. He accomplished this by doing everything His Father and the Holy Spirit told Him to do. He always lived in truth regardless of how He felt (Luke 22:42). Jesus wanted to bring glory to His Father, and that is exactly what He desires for you too. That's why Jesus told His disciples, "I am the vine, you are the branches; he who abides [communes] in Me and I in him, he bears much fruit, for apart from Me you can do nothing" (John 15:5). Jesus is saying that, without abiding in Him, no one can bring glory to the Father. Moreover, no one abides in Jesus without living in truth, for He is the Truth (John 14:6).

You must be holy to see Jesus face to face (1 Peter 1:16). You don't deny the obstacles in your race, and when you pass through them, you don't look back; you look forward. When driving a car, you don't look out the back window to go forward. You press on toward the goal of practical holiness, which is what the Holy Spirit uses the obstacles to produce (Romans 5:3–5).

The apostle Paul had much to regret in his past. He persecuted the church and was involved in imprisoning (Acts 8:3, 22:4, 26:10) and killing (Acts 7:58, 26:10) Christians. But look at the positive and negative aspects of what he tells us in Philippians 3:13: "Brothers, I do not consider myself as having laid hold of it yet, but one thing I do: forgetting what lies behind and reaching forward to what lies ahead." To live in truth, you must choose to forget your past (negative) and reach forward to what lasts forever (positive). When you look back while moving forward, you will be unstable (James 1:8). Instability is an obstacle to running that you can avoid by keeping your eyes fixed on the finish line ahead (Christlikeness). Solomon instructs us to, "Look straight ahead, and fix your eyes on what lies before you. Mark out a straight path for your feet; stay on the safe path. Don't get sidetracked; keep your feet from following evil" (Proverbs 4:25–27, NLT).

Not looking back means avoiding the disasters caused by past sins committed against you and by you, and also avoiding dwelling on past victories. Both are stumbling blocks to finishing the race and will enslave you. Choose not to let your past victories or defeats control your present and future choices. The clearest vision for finishing your race is to stay laser-focused on Jesus. Keep in mind Jesus' warning in Luke 9:62, "But Jesus said to him, 'No one, after putting his hand to the plow and looking back, is fit for the kingdom of God.'" You don't become like Jesus while looking backward.

You must learn to speak the truth to yourself—words of kindness, comfort, and encouragement. This is part of being God's child and temple (John 1:12; 1 Corinthians 3:16). God wants you to run the race with an accurate understanding of who you are in Christ (Galatians 2:20). Throughout each day, remind yourself of the following truths from the book of Ephesians, as God has already blessed you with them.

He has...

1. blessed you with every spiritual blessing in the heavenly places in Christ (1:3).

2. chosen, predestined, and adopted you as His child (1:4–5).

3. lavished you with His grace (1:6, 8, 2:7).

4. redeemed and forgiven you (1:7, 4:32).

5. given you the mystery of His will (1:9–10).

6. made you a receiver of an inheritance (1:11).

7. sealed you with the Holy Spirit (1:13–14, 4:30).

8. greatly loved you (2:4, 5:25).

9. made you alive with new life (2:5–7).

10. made you the workmanship of Christ created by Him for doing good works (2:10).

11. given you His own peace (2:14).

12. made you one with Christ and with every believer as His own body (2:13–19, 3:4–6).

13. made you a citizen of His kingdom and a member of His family (2:19).

14. built you into His own temple and the dwelling place of His Spirit (2:20–22).

15. given you boldness and confident access to God (3:12).

16. made you powerful beyond your imagination (3:19–20).

17. given you the unity of the Spirit in the bond of peace (4:1–3).

18. individually and uniquely gifted you through Christ (4:7).

19. blessed you with specially-gifted leaders to equip you in the work of ministry (4:11–12).

20. taught you Christ (4:20–21).

21. given you a new self in God's holy likeness (4:24).

Notice how the apostle Paul describes himself in Philippians 3:12–14 (NLT):

I don't mean to say that I have already achieved these things or that I have already reached perfection. But I press on to possess that perfection for which Christ Jesus first possessed me. No, dear brothers and sisters, I have not achieved it, but I focus on this one thing: Forgetting the past and looking forward to what lies ahead, I press on to reach the end of the race and receive the heavenly prize for which God, through Christ Jesus, is calling us.

In some ways, we are like Paul. We know about the many spiritual blessings promised to us, but we haven't yet achieved the practical holiness we desire. We need to imitate Paul and keep pressing on to the end of our race. He also instructs us on what to focus on as we run our race: "So we don't look at the troubles we can see now; rather, we fix our gaze on things that cannot be seen. For the things we see now will soon be gone, but the things we cannot see will last forever" (2 Corinthians 4:18, NLT). In other words, as you run your spiritual steeplechase, don't look down or back at the obstacles on your path, for Paul tells you that they will soon no longer exist. All the obstacles in your life will soon be gone. Instead, focus on what you can't yet see but know exists. So, how do you focus on something you can't see? You are to run each day, telling yourself the truth of these spiritual blessings. For now, we run by faith, but one day you will live unhampered in the freedom of the truth. Amen.

I encourage you to listen to the song "Redeemed" by Big Daddy Weave (2012).

ABOUT THE AUTHOR

Michael F. Sabo, PhD, previously directed the Navigator Collegiate Ministry at Bowling Green State University in Ohio. As a Navigator, he pioneered the introduction of discipleship instruction in seminaries. He has served as a pastor and an adjunct faculty member at Trinity Evangelical Divinity School in Deerfield, Illinois, and at Denver Seminary in Littleton, Colorado.

In 2001, Michael became the founder and president of Christian Leadership Institute (CLI), an alternative to traditional seminary. CLI trains pastors in Tanzania how to do inductive Bible study, develop expository sermons, and disciple others.

Michael and his wife, Darlene, live in Colorado Springs, Colorado, where they serve at a local church, lead Bible studies, and teach the homeless at the Springs Rescue Mission. They have four children and four grandchildren.

To contact Michael, please visit the CLI website at https://christian leadership.institute.

The Christian Leadership Institute (CLI) is a Christian ministry offering a creative and holistic alternative to traditional seminary education. Rather than the traditional lecture-based approach to biblical content and testing, CLI uses a teaching format that includes seven creative instructional methods. These include Learning Communities, Spiritual Transformation Groups, Mentoring, Counseling, Family Gatherings, Apprenticeships, and Cross-cultural Training. Instead of written tests, students develop learning contracts.

CLI also offers training for local church leaders and Christians, tailored to each church's needs. For more details on each format and our international training, please visit our website at https://christianleadership.institute

Mission Statement
To collectively unite the training strengths of seminaries,
local churches, and parachurch ministries, resulting in the
holistic development of godly leaders.

Vision Statement
To develop Christian Leaders who have a strong love for God, a growing
godly character, and a high level of biblical and ministry competence.

Core Values
Loving God is Foundational
Loving Others is Essential
Humility is Needed
Holiness is Central
Integrity is Paramount
Obedience is Required
Biblical Scholarship is Imperative

Statement of Faith
See website

NOTES

INTRODUCTION: THE BASIS OF CHRISTIAN FREEDOM

i. Kinlaw, D. F. *This Day with the Master: 365 Daily Meditations*, "A Pledge to Truth," (Grand Rapids, MI: Zondervan, 2023).

2. FREEDOM OF THE WILL

i. Sproul, R. C. *Willing to Believe: The Controversy over Free Will*. (Ada, MI: Baker Books, 1997), 34.
ii. Ibid, 155.
iii. Ibid.
iv. Ibid.
v. Ibid, 156.
vi. Ibid.
vii. Ibid.
viii. Ibid.
ix. Ibid, 158.
x. Ibid, 158.
xi. Ibid.
xii. Ibid.
xiii. Ibid.
xiv. Ibid.
xv. Ibid, 160.
xvi. Ibid, 168.
xvii. Ibid, 165.
xviii. Ibid.
xix. Arthur Bennett, *The Valley of Vision*, "Belonging to Jesus," (Edinburgh: Banner of Truth Trust, 1975).
xx. *The Matrix* is a 1999 science fiction action film written and directed by the Wachowski brothers.

3. FREEDOM THROUGH A RENEWED MIND

i. From the online *Guideposts* Classics / reprinted July 24, 2014, by Corrie ten Boom. I suggest you read the entire online article.
ii. Anderson, N. T. *Discipleship Counseling*, (Corsicana, TX: Regal Books, 2003), 91.

4. FREEDOM FROM GUILT

i. Wolgemuth, N. D., & Tada, J. E. *Choosing Gratitude: Your Journey to Joy* (Chicago, IL: Moody Publishers, 2009), 35.

5. FREEDOM FROM WORRY

i. MacArthur, J. F., Jr. *Grace to You: John MacArthur Sermon Archive*, 2014.
ii. Lucado, M. *Less Fret, More Faith: An 11-Week Action Plan to Overcome Anxiety.* (Nashville, TN: Thomas Nelson, 2017).
iii. Hunt, June. *Worry, The Joy Stealer.* (Torrance, CA: Aspire Press: 2021), 15.
iv. Nouwen, Henri. *The Heart of Nouwen,* edited by Rebecca Laird and Michael J. Christensen, (Spring Valley, New York: Crossroad, 2003).
v. Hull, Bill. *Right Thinking*, (Colorado Springs, CO: NavPress, 1985), 66.
vi. Stott, John. *Your Mind Matters*, (Downers Grove, IL: InterVarsity, 1972), 16.
vii. Lloyd-Jones, D. Martyn. *Studies in the Sermon on the Mount,* (Grand Rapids, MI: Eerdmans, 1971), 129–130.

6. FREEDOM FROM PRIDE

i. Oswalt, J. N. *The Book of Isaiah,* (Grand Rapids, MI: Eerdmans Publishing Co., 1986), 320-321.
ii. Wiersbe, W. W. *Be Comforted,* (Colorado Springs, CO: Victor Books, 1996), 44-46.
iii. MacArthur, J. F., Jr. *Philippians*, (Chicago, IL: Moody Press, 2001), 129.
iv. Ibid, 132.
v. John Piper. *Battling Unbelief*, (Sisters, OR: Multnomah, 2007), 41-42.
vi. Ibid, 49.
vii. Ibid, 50.

7. FREEDOM FROM FEAR

i. Demir, G.T., Namlı, S., Çakır, E. *et al.* The role of mental toughness, sport imagery and anxiety in athletic performance: structural equation modelling analysis. *BMC Psychol* 13, 869 (2025). https://doi.org/10.1186/s40359-025-03250-6.
ii. Flavel, John. *Triumphing over Sinful Fear,* (Grand Rapids, MI: Reformation Heritage Books, 2022), viii.
iii. Ibid, 8.
iv. Ibid.
v. Ibid, 14-15.
vi. Ibid, 17.
vii. MacArthur, J. F., Jr. (2014). *Grace to You: John MacArthur Sermon Archive.*

8. FREEDOM FROM UNRIGHTEOUS ANGER

i. Boice, J. M. *Psalms 107–150: An Expositional Commentary,* (Ada, MI: Baker Books, 2005), 974.
ii. Reyburn, W. D., & Fry, E. M. *A Handbook on Proverbs,* (England: United Bible Societies, 2000), 321-322.
iii. Baker, W., & Carpenter, E. E. *The Complete Word Study Dictionary: Old Testament,* (Chattanooga, TN: AMG Publishers, 2003), 83.
iv. Wright, J. R. *Proverbs, Ecclesiastes, Song of Solomon,* (Lisle, IL: InterVarsity Press, 2005), 101.
v. Pierre, Jeremy, *Tabletalk*, June 2022, 9.

9. FREEDOM FROM LONELINESS

    i. Miller, Calvin. *The Table Of Inwardness,* (Lisle, IL: InterVarsity Press, 1984), 18.

    ii. Ibid.

    iii. Ibid, 19.

    iv. Boice, J. M. *Psalms 107–150: An Expositional Commentary,* (Ada, MI: Baker Books, 2005), 1,228-1,229.

    v. Ibid.

    vi. Ibid, 1,229

    vii. Keller, T. *Walking with God Through Pain and Suffering,* (Boston, MA; Dutton, 2013), 5.

    viii. Elliot, Elisabeth. Three-part message series on *Loneliness.* This quote is from her third message subtitled *Something to Offer God.*

    ix. Elliot, Elisabeth. Three-part message series on *Loneliness.* This quote is from her second message subtitled *In Acceptance Lieth Peace.*

    x. Ibid.

    xi. Wiersbe, W. W. *With the Word Bible Commentary,* (Nashville, TN: Thomas Nelson, 1991).

    xii. Boice, J. M. *Psalms 107–150: An Expositional Commentary,* (Ada, MI: Baker Books, 2005), 107-150.

    xiii. Ibid, 1,230.

10. FREEDOM TO WORSHIP GOD IN SPIRIT AND TRUTH

    i. Garrett, D. A. *Hosea, Joel,* (Nashville, TN: Broadman & Holman Publishers, 1997), 161.

    ii. Simeon, C. *Horae Homileticae: Hosea to Malachi,* (Holdsworth and Ball, 1832), 61-62.

    iii. Kittel, G., Friedrich, G., & Bromiley, G. W. *Theological Dictionary of the New Testament, Abridged in One Volume,* (Grand Rapids, MI: Eerdmans, 1985), 2.

ENDING WITH A RACE

    i. Kinlaw, D. F. *This Day with the Master: 365 Daily Meditations,* "A Pledge to Truth," (Grand Rapids, MI: Zondervan, 2023).

    ii. Sabo, Michael Frank, *The Responsible Christian,* (April 1979).